The
of Life

*Allow yourself to hear what
vibrates inside you*

FRANÇOISE RAMBAUD

CP
THE CHOIR PRESS

First published in the United Kingdom in 2023 by
The Choir Press

ISBN 978-1-78963-367-2

Our thoughts, like our actions, emit vibrations.

It is up to each individual to find his or her own frequency.

Grow, learn from life and love.

This is what I want to say to my grandchildren and to you, the reader.

Life's only demand is to be practised, to be lived; and it is our duty to maintain this with humility.

Preface

I am writing this book to communicate with parents but also their children. As a child, we don't always understand what is going on around us. Nowadays, I meet a lot of children who have experienced very strong moments, like having visions, children with powerful feelings and emotions. They see things, feel things but they don't dare talk about it, simply because they are not heard.

As a child I went through this exact situation. And I don't know where I got the energy to carry on … Fortunately, at the age of seven, I could hear deep from within myself: 'I am the only one who knows what is best for me'. This affirmation, that I could hear all the time, formed a strength; and to this day, this affirmation is my strength. In this book, I want to transmit the teaching I received throughout my life, and what I acquire still today. I had the chance at different times in my life to cross paths with great mentors, but also life itself offered me great teaching.

In other words, through all my life experiences, I stayed true and faithful to myself.

Transmission

Surrounded by the warm light of the forest which I have just entered; my being is back to its source. I am sitting on a soft carpet of green moss, the air is fresh, I feel good. In the mist of the forest, I connect myself to the All Living. I am calling my allies, the kind spirits that are all present around me. I sing. The sky. The moon. I play my drum. The trees. The birds. The stones. The spirits … they are all my friends. I stay within the silence of the forest, which is nothing but silent. I am grateful for its welcome homecoming; I feel its force coming to me. The emptiness in my being transforms itself into a friendly force. The silence of inner peace takes over my being. I sing again, drumming. Now I know what I must do. I go and meet the people I left a few minutes ago.

It is Sunday, late afternoon, in Poland. I was feeling a bit withdrawn with a group I was watching during a seminar, so I went away into the forest. The group was satisfied with the seminar, but I was not. Today is the last day.

Back in the room, I meet all these people with whom I shared some beautiful moments. It is time to say goodbye. But a force, from within, tells me that I can't let them go yet. So, before they leave, I ask them to form a line, one behind one another. I am facing them. I open my arms.

At the exact time at which I open my arms, I express a simple demand, and call my allies, my spirits. The energy rising in me becomes more and more powerful. A strength is driven towards all the men and women facing me. The reactions are immediate. A storm of emotions invades the room we are in. Each and every one of them reacts in their own way: laughter, screaming, sickness, tears …

Behind me, one of the windows shatters. The ceiling cracks. And I see a candle going out. Time, for an instant, seems to pause. Don't look for an understanding. By going deep inside myself, I removed the roots that were holding us back, preventing us from breathing, and I offered them this energy as a benevolent wave.

I am only a transmission.

Freedom of Speech During Childhood

Only I know what is good for me. Only a little girl, I was saying this to my parents, my teachers, the church sisters. *Only I know what is good for me.* "Take your jumper! You are going to be cold." Who else apart from myself, knows if I am going to be cold or if I am going to be hot? Who else needs to order me around, to explain what is better for me?

A lot of people can think the same thing. On the other hand, what I feel, what I have inside, I am the only one to feel it.

Listen to your heart, listen to yourself! Listen to this vibration that makes you alive.

As a little girl, I didn't know that … I knew. So, I said everything! To everybody! But when I was twelve, I was taken to the village priest, and then to an exorcist … they wanted to detain me. Yes, detain me in a special hospital. I stopped telling what I felt, what I saw, what I heard. From that moment on, I started to distrust the grownups, but I carried on listening, feeling the invisible world.

The invisible is here. We don't know how to see it, or we don't want to see it.

When I think of myself as a kid, the first image that comes to me is anger. A black energy coming. I see myself with my school blouse, and this black energy, anger, is there. I can hear, "You have some attitude, you." Yes, that's right, but it is you, the grownups, who think I am crazy, who lie to me. Yes, you the grownups, who, with your judgments and your fears, build what I am.

I am angry because I know you are lying to me, they lie. This thought that I had when I was a little girl, seven years old, forged my strength. Today, when I talk about it with my uncle, who is eighty-six, he has this look towards me, and he remembers: "We couldn't understand you. You were a mystery." And slowly, he adds, "We thought you were inhabited by the devil." They didn't understand me, and I didn't understand them. Two worlds, two universes, the same in fact, but different keys. I had access to the invisible world, and I thought everyone could see the same as I. But more than once, I was brought back to their reality, their universe.

On most Sundays, the family got together for a Sunday meal. On one Sunday in particular, a large number of the family were sitting at the table where we ate and drank. At one point, around the table, the adults started discussing an aunt who had recently passed on. They talked about her jewellery and some paper-work. Nobody knew where they were, they couldn't find anything! But if only they could find this jewellery and this paperwork, it would help everyone. So I asked: "Why don't you ask her?" And because it seemed as though they couldn't hear me, I repeated: "Why don't you ask her? Just ask her, she is right here." I was only a kid, I didn't know that there were certain things you were not meant to say. The conversation stopped. Everyone was looking at me, some with round eyes, some frowning, some rolling their eyes. And then I was dragged to the kitchen. Punished. But what had I done?

Punished. But what had I done?

When our neighbour, Pepe Constant, passed away, when my grandmother Julie died, I told the adults. Both came to me to say goodbye before they left. I was telling people before they knew it themselves. I was, no doubt, 'rewarded' by a slap again.

The aunt, she was there, in front of me, I saw her. 'Why don't you ask her, where the jewellery and paperwork are?' Be quiet! Stop talking nonsense! After being isolated in the kitchen, after being punished, once the storm eventually calmed down, someone was finally ready to listen to what I had to say. "I know where the jewellery and paperwork are. Aunty told me." So, half scared, half sceptical, they went to the hidden place I told them about, towards an old wooden piece of furniture. Everything was there: jewellery and paperwork.

From that moment on, did my family look at me with a

funny eye, half scared, half intrigued? Remember, I was eight years old. Children are spontaneous, and even if it is the truth, it can be, most of the time, very hard to hear.

I don't think I was easy as a child. Already, at the age of six, I would wander away, go for a walk on my own. Being too small to know my way around the streets, I would get home eventually, when I was ready to go home. Every time, I was welcomed back with, "Where have you been? I was looking for you everywhere! I was worried sick! You don't realise!" In my own words, I tried to explain who I was. Grownups project their fear, it is not mine, this fear does not belong to me. I told them: "This is your fear, not mine."

I never had the feeling of being put aside; however, I was considered by some adults to be a pest. My cousins were, for a time, not allowed to play with me.

My parents must have been worried about this strange child that was sometimes found talking to herself. My dad often told me: "We don't know what to do with you!" A blurry memory comes back to me. Kneeling, so that he could be at the same height as me, he repeats: "You should not say that, you must not say that." My mum was behind us and I could feel her anguish. I could almost hear what she was thinking: *But what are we going to do with her?* My parents' reaction seemed completely dis-proportional, even violent, compared to what I had done. This image of my dad, feeling helpless, repeating, "You must not say that."

Today, I am aware that I told a truth, a hidden truth; I can't really remember which one. Maybe, it was while speaking to our

neighbour. I told her about the violence she was living with at home. Or maybe it was about Caroline? As a child, nothing could surprise me, therefore I was not surprised to see in my house a little girl that everybody kept ignoring. When I mentioned it to one of my neighbours, he was the one to be stunned: "Why are you talking about this child? Little Caroline, nobody talks about her anymore ... she died years ago." Well, Caroline, I could see her, I could hear her.

Years later, when we were living in this house, Caroline appeared to my daughter, Pauline. Pauline was nine years old, and during the night she could hear the girl who had disappeared. Pauline did not feel safe, was always disturbed by this invisible presence. So, we lit a candle, and very simply, we asked Caroline to leave us in peace. By this very simple ritual, Caroline's presence faded away and Pauline found peace again. She could now fall asleep without worrying.

At school, apart from my conversations with myself, everything was going well. I was a very studious pupil until one day, in secondary school, during a parent-teacher meeting, one of my teachers told my parents that I had real academic potential. I could progress up the levels very quickly. I told my teacher that I was not interested (I was aware that this academic knowledge would not be any use to me). He looked at me and very carefully thought about his next words. "Yes, but that's what becoming adult means. It is time to grow up and be serious." *OK, but this is exactly what I don't want!* "If I become serious, it means I will become like you, thanks but no thanks. I don't want to be like you. I don't want to become serious." Saying that to my teacher sounded like a prophecy. No, I didn't want to become serious. From that meeting, my schooling changed. I did as little as possible.

What to do with a child who has the devil in her? My uncle reminds me today: "We didn't know what to do with you." In order to deal with their worries, the adults tried to 'heal' me, with whatever means they had. They sent me to speak with the priest. Every Sunday, my parents went to church, my father played music during Mass. And sometimes, the priest would come and have lunch at our house. I would tell them: "Jesus didn't ask for all this."

"And how do you know?"

"Because he told me." It is totally unthinkable, in this Catholic background, to let a child speak such stupidity as that. The priest tried his best, but I held on. Eventually the priest didn't know what to do anymore, so we went towards Luçon, a nearby town. Maybe the exorcist of the area would know how to deal with this situation.

I have only vague memories of this meeting. The exorcist

appeared to me like a black mass, an entity that wanted to dominate me. He tried using incense, chants and gentle taps on the head. He tried. He did his act of exorcism. This priest (huge, to my eyes) wished for me to deny what I represented, who I was. This man, dressed all in black, reminded me of the devil. He didn't know that he was actually reinforcing my convictions, feeding my anger; that anger that made me feel alive. The more I moved forward in my childhood, the more I understood that the world I saw, was not theirs to see. A huge part of what I sensed was forbidden to them, they couldn't see it. It was invisible. It is true that I had the habit of telling the priest as well as the sisters at my school: "What you are saying is a lie! Jesus was a man like any other! He didn't walk on water, he didn't … Jesus was a man like any other." Of course, this kind of talk kept getting me into trouble, punishments of all kinds, slaps on demand. The love of your neighbour must slip through the sisters' hands! My speeches about Jesus did not really go with my Communion dress. My parents must have been really worried. During my Communion, we preached unconditional love. We had to be love. I found it really hard to understand this love coming from a person who had just given me a slap. This love they were preaching did not fit with reality. I knew who I was. So when they talked about unconditional love, it made me angry. This emotion, this energy, helped me deal with the adult world, until …

The meeting with the exorcist didn't change me. Coming back from this encounter, at only eight years old, I smiled. Because in this visible world, at least the one I perceived, I felt, right beside me, my two friends. They have been by my side, since I was very small, since I can remember, since forever. We always exchange stories, we chit-chat. I always have great fun with them. Uriel and Jesus are my mates. Their presence warms my body and my soul, and they teach me, they share some of their knowledge with me, petite Francoise.

I always had what people would call signs. As a child, I never tried to interpret them, and if I found them hard to understand, I found it even harder to make them understandable to others. If I liked getting dressed for Mass, it is only because I wanted more than anything to become a spiritual healer, which I knew did not really go well with the Catholic dogma. So, as the child that I was, I played along with all these rituals, especially when we were supposed to stay sensible. The Path of the Cross, long and tedious, bored me so much. What I loved, was life, yes, the singing, the chants, the hymn; I loved them. But on the other hand, I found it very hard to stay serious, especially during the ceremonies. A few of my then friends must remember our Communion.

We are all dressed in our white dresses and a veil covering our hair, ready for our Sunday Communion, when I am thinking about spicing it up a bit. When we are sitting down, the material of our headdress hangs quite low, almost touching the floor. The girl in front of me has a headdress that calls for my attention. When she comes and sits down once more, I put a pin in her veil, fixing it to the chair. When she gets up again, we hear screaming. The veil is still on the chair. The young girl find herself veil-less. The sister who is on duty that day very quickly intervenes and I get punished again.

So I kept saying what I saw, what I felt, until one day ... I closed myself. I was twelve years old. Because the exorcism did not work, the grownups found another solution. What was there apart from religion? Science ... and just like that, we hopped into the car and headed to a psychiatrist. I know things, I perceive things intimately. In the invisible, a path lights up with every step we take, and with every step Destiny draws itself. From a very young age, I developed this consciousness: I know who I am. Nothing scares me. But when I met with this psychiatrist, I knew I needed to protect myself. I was twelve years old, I kept on reading the invisible and also talking about it. I spoke to myself about all sorts of things, some that might test rationality. In my school ground, crouching, I asked Francoise: 'Can you help me with the test after the break?' Sister Louise, a very caring person, asked me who I was talking to. I explained that I was talking to Francoise: I am a lot of Francoise. Obviously, even with all her good will, Sister Louise did not quite understand me.

So when I hear the psychiatrist saying to my parents: "If she keeps going, we will have to intern her," I understand. I am twelve years old, and I need to protect myself, I must keep quiet. The invisible world will keep coming to visit me if it wants to, but for my part, I will not speak of it anymore. I will try my best to not say anything ... until the age of thirty-three.

I keep all these things inside until ...

The Dolce Vita

I should have suspected that something, how do I say this ... from beyond, was calling me out, tickling me. At school, during my first year (CP), my teachers asked me: "What do you want to be when you grow up?" I replied: "Me, I want to be a spiritual healer." Clearly not the kind of answer she was expecting. This is however what I replied to my teacher who stayed speechless. I was inhabited by a strong intuition that was growing and making itself stronger and stronger without me really noticing. For example, when, a few years later, I bought an encyclopaedia, instead of buying *Tout l'Univers* like everybody else, I bought *The Encyclopaedia of Beyond*!

As a small child, I always had this feeling of being punished all the time. I loved staring into the night, at the stars and observing the magical sky. And I kept staring at it and repeating: 'I want to go home ...' Being here, on Planet Earth, I often had that feeling of being punished. And then, little by little, the idea that I am here for a reason started to grow; I am here because I need to do something. I need to find my place. It is probably for that reason that as a teenager I never missed an opportunity to have adventures. With a few friends, I went to Rouen for a few days. Without telling anyone. On my return, I was obviously rewarded by a huge telling off. But I didn't care; I chose life.

When I was eighteen, I went to work in Val-Thorens in the French Alps. At the end of the season, I went to the train station to catch my train back home to Vendee. Except that once at the train station, while having a look at the train timetable, I noticed that Viareggio was cheaper than going home. So, what did I do? I got a ticket to Viareggio. No need to tell my parents; let's go! But once I arrived at my destination, very quickly things became complicated. I got my bag stolen; everything I owned, clothes, passport, the lot. I found myself all alone in Italy. I would stay there for eight months.

I learnt so much during that time: how to handle things on my own, beg for food and money, share whatever we had with some friends I made that were in the same situation. We didn't really need anything, and we actually didn't lack for anything. I asked myself this question: maybe that's the real life? I took the days as they came without asking about tomorrow. My freedom became my only luggage. I thanked myself for living through these moments. I experienced strong solidarity in this total freedom. One day, by coincidence, I met some French people on a camp site. We talked, and slowly, I started to feel homesick; but I decided to not let this feeling take control and decided to travel south. I got to Naples.

I kept learning, a lot. I met an Italian, the very handsome Emilio. He let me enter his 'family'. And I just kept learning. On the material side of things, everything was different, no need to beg from the restaurant's kitchen. I discovered the beautiful life. The dolce vita. I was in the inner circle, champagne, petit fours. I found myself in the opposite of my previous life: out of the street into opulence!

Just like in a movie, everything rolled at 100 miles per hour, the intoxication of speed won me over. Money, loads of money, everywhere. I even had bodyguards to go shopping, every time I went out … In this circle, everything went very fast, and like a lot of people around me, I could succumb at any time. Drugs, sex and rock 'n' roll, I saw a lot of friends sinking.

One evening, my friend and I went to one of their parties, and after a while I realised that she had disappeared. I started to look for her. I asked the guests if anyone had seen Blandine, but nothing. Finally, I saw a hidden door that opened and from the darkness, Blandine came out. I started approaching her, but after her came a man. Even though the light was very dim, it was not hard to see that this man was far from being our age. Blandine lowered her head, tried to smile and her eyes avoided me. She needed money quickly to get her next fix. She was selling her body. Her beautiful big blue eyes observed me. She was so taken by the drugs, she even injected herself under her tongue, because her arms couldn't take it anymore.

Later, I helped her to free herself from her cage. Heroin has a strong hold, and damages everything. Blandine was OK, she managed to get away from it all. These moments were very strong, full of great strength, great power. Everything made people fall around me; sex, drugs, but I was never tempted; I didn't fall into the traps. I had an envelope of protection around

9

me. I unconsciously felt dangers, what was right and what was less right. This way of life couldn't last forever. I found myself emotionally in complete opposition to all the violence around me. I have it in myself, this strong desire to save abused, beaten people, and therefore I helped my friend get clean and detoxify, not without pain and anguish. But I was not scared.

However, there came a time when I realised I was not free. One day, we were all in the kitchen (in Italy, the kitchen is a woman's place). I started guessing a story that was kept hidden from me. I started to understand throughout our conversations that this woman, who I had recently noticed, was Emilio's official wife! And me? I was Francesca and what else? From that moment on, I wanted to run away. I was eighteen and all my life was ahead of me.

When I decided to leave, people around me made me understand that we couldn't get out of this kind of circle that easily. One of the bodyguards, luckily, must have had a crush on me. Seeing me in this difficult position he understood and offered his help. But we had to be extremely discreet. One day, he managed to make me climb into the boot of one the cars, with strict orders not to move. He drove out of the estate and brought me to a safe place. He hid me in a house, forbidding me to move, to give them enough time to forget me. He left me with food and very strict instructions: I was not allowed to open the shutters nor turn the light on. Nobody must notice my presence in this house, which should be empty.

I knew that I was protected. I felt this deep faith that nothing could happen to me. Once he realised that the danger had passed, the bodyguard who put me in the safe house took me to a police station. From there, I explained that my passport had been stolen ... I could also call my parents. My father, who had not seen me in over a year, without any news, came and got me. And I finally went back to France.

Throughout my time in Italy, not once was I scared. I never felt myself in any danger; I had the feeling of living life to the full and for me, it was an amazing experience. For that matter, I was just back home when I wanted to go on my next adventure. I felt I needed to meet more people, experience life even more. In later years, I would not fail to hear: "You were an adventurer, your parents must have seen it all." I just wanted to have passion in my life. Subconsciously, I knew that if I was to be on this planet, it was to experiment. I felt very different from all my friends.

I experimented with life and I had fun. Nothing stopped me. I chose to live life to the full. I believed nothing could stop me. How many times was I told that I was foolish? But I didn't have the feeling of being foolish, I was always able to recognise danger. When I chose to live life to the full, I didn't care about being punished; at least I chose. I made a choice; I listened to myself, and I was present in that moment.

That year in Italy did not prevent me from continuing to live my life.

At twenty-one, I was pregnant with Julie. I started a family with Bruno, we got married. We have three children: Julie born in 1980, Antoine in 1983 and Pauline in 1985. And to date, I have eight grandchildren. Just like me, they perceive a lot of things, each with their own characteristics. In order of appearance: Ethan, Lola, Kyle, Tia, Willow, Eden, Avana and Scarlett. The last one dances with life; she is a guardian of the earth.

To each of them to find their place and listen to the world.

From Paralysis to Life

I keep everything to myself until …

I am thirty-three years old. That door, that I am trying so hard to keep shut, opens suddenly. It gives in. Everything I was trying to hide bursts out into the open, a violent eruption pins me down. The energy that I had been suppressing, since I was twelve years old, crystallised and in the process of freeing itself, nearly killed me.

I kept all these things secret and invisible. Locked deep inside, until …

On one bizarre day, an event happened to me, that questioned all my faith and made me think: *If that happens to me … well, I have no doubt something to understand.*

For a while, I had been feeling as if pins and needles were invading my body, as if, little by little, a paralysis was seizing me. First the eye, then the arm, and so forth; my right side often felt as though it was blocked, even my leg. The paralysis progressed gradually. Sometimes, it was hard to walk, but generally I managed to do whatever needed to be done. My GP warned me: "Be careful." But I kept telling myself that it was OK, there was surely a good reason behind all this … I would find out.

So, I kept going, as best I could, until … I was in my car, driving. I came to a junction in the city centre of Jard-sur-Mer. I saw the stop sign, and then suddenly, nothing. It was as if the sign wanted to tell me something. I found myself at the wheel, unable to move, completely locked from the inside. My entire right side was completely paralysed. Blocked. Because my car was now stationary, near a shop, very quickly passers-by noticed the car and the immobile driver … I couldn't move, I couldn't do anything, only endure. One of the shopkeepers called for help, an ambulance was on its way.

On my way to the hospital, my GP had already arranged for an emergency appointment with the neurologist. Once there, I went through all the tests possible (I can still see myself with the electrodes head cap). Aneurism? Multiple sclerosis? They needed to know what was going on … the smell of the hospital got to me, I started being sick, and again, and again. I was sick everywhere, in the lift, on my bed. Despite all the tests, the doctors were perplexed. I was in my hospital bed with all these movements around me. I smiled. Even though I felt frozen, I felt everything. I heard everything. But there was nothing I could do; I was nailed to my bed. The doctors then decided to do a lumbar puncture. They came to me with this big needle, and they started. I just had enough time to tell Bruno, my husband, who was standing beside me: "I am going."

I had this very clear vision. I was above my body. I left them to their agitations and moved towards a long tunnel. I felt sucked in at a very fast speed. I went through a place with loads of faces. I was coming to a bright place; I felt myself surrounded by a feeling of wellbeing. I felt a gentle, soft warmth, something very comforting. I felt great.

Except that … I couldn't stay here. I understood that very quickly. A bright density, very bright … an entity held me by the shoulders. Without being too dazzling, the place where I was seemed to be full to the brim with light. I surrendered myself to this light. Despite all this abundance that I felt, I seemed to understand that I could not stay. This bright presence came even closer, I could feel it stronger than before. I had to choose, going back … or not. I felt so good here. A real struggle shook my entire soul. I was torn between attraction and revulsion, between being sucked in by that light, or going back to where I came from. So I decided. I thought I knew what was hindering me. I still had things to do on Earth. I was being asked to go back down. Yet, I felt so good here! Yes, certainly, but I still had something to accomplish. OK. I chose. And I chose life.

A little reluctantly, but reassured by what I felt, I came back. I lived again …

When I was coming back down, I was determined not to hang around the hospital … my paralysis had disappeared. I explained to the hospital staff what I had been through and immediately they send me to a psychiatrist. "We will give you some medication, Ma'am!" I signed my discharge; I wanted out of there as quickly as possible. With Bruno, we went back home. Once home, I knew something new was offering itself to me. OK, I have something to do, but what? Ask life and life will show you the way. Yes, but realistically? So, every day I asked, what can I do? And I stayed there with this question hanging.

I felt very isolated by the experience I had just been through. People who go through the same or similar experience do not talk about it. It was only the start of the nineties, and this sort of experience was kept a secret. People did not dare talk about it.

A little while after my experience at the hospital, terrible news come to knock on my door. My brother phoned me to tell me that his son, who was just born, was in a critical situation. He was in intensive care and in great danger. According to the doctors, his son had only five days to live. A serious respiratory problem that left the baby no chance of survival. My nephew was condemned? Just born, and already lost?

I hung up, stunned by the information. Even today, I can still hear myself: *What can I do? Tell me?* So intuitively, I do something. For a few hours, I kneel, moving my hands, making movement. I fall to the floor, and I perform like I feel, like I can. Incapable of describing what I am doing, but I am doing it. What movements? What sounds? I don't know but I do them.

The day after, my brother called me, his voice has changed. His son is saved!

Take a Lesson

How to define who I am? I can claim to this day that saving souls is, without a doubt, what makes me vibrate from my childhood. But before I started saving souls, I understood I first needed to learn to look after myself. Saving does not mean sacrificing yourself for others. It is necessary to love yourself before turning to others.

I would not know how to define myself.

Maybe my daughter, Pauline, found the words that resonated the most, that sounded clearer. We both went to Poland for a workshop, where I taught regularly. On our way back, after seeing me doing what I do, Pauline had these words: "In fact, you perform energetic surgery!" Yes, I work with my hands, I compose with them, I twirl them. A bit like a musician who uses his instrument but with the idea of healing. I do movements very close to the person. I look to channel the person's energy, in order to direct it to the best place.

During a workshop, I accompany the participants, I see the invisible. I can detect everything that envelops these people. So, with my hands, I pull, I push, I get rid of 'stuff'. My movements are very precise. In every workshop, each and every one of the participants reacts one way or another. Each their own way, depending on the energies that are present. Some start having a coughing fit, others are sick, others cry, scream, laugh or all of these emotions at the same time. Following each of my interventions, the person has a reaction. I do only a very simple movement but each movement is very close to them, close to their soul.

Before I started teaching, I travelled a long path, I met some wonderful teachers. Life knew, in its own way, how to teach me beautifully.

The first majestic lesson, at thirty-three, the paralysis hit me, and could have left me on the floor. It was enough to stop me there, to bury me. No. I continued to live on, even if my entourage got scared. Pauline, my daughter, had a very strong feeling. When I was in the ER, that day, paralysed, Pauline was in school. At that instant, her teacher came close to her to ask her what was going on. Pauline was in tears. "Pauline, what is going on? Why are you crying?"

"My mum is dying."

"Don't be silly, I saw your mum this morning and everything was fine." It was only when she got home that she found out how true her feeling was, how close I was to not coming back. She remembers it very well; emotional memory is very powerful.

After my 'awakening' at thirty-three, I listened more than ever to everything the world was telling me, I listened to myself. I also looked. I built myself up around reiki, and also travelled to India, Nepal and South America. I went to visit all these countries where I met wonderful masters who guided me. These great initiatory travels started with dreams, like all the big decisions that marked my life. I am not going into detail about all the teachings I have had, as you really need to experience them, but I will tell you about the moments that were most powerful.

First Step

After this indescribable moment, that science tries to label 'near death experience', I feel different, really different from the person I was before. I need to know more. My thirst for knowledge grows. At the time, I was going through a tsunami of emotions; nobody talks about this sort of thing.

I needed to know more. It was as if the door that opened was still calling me. I wanted to see more. I asked for the universe to send me signs, send me people to guide me towards this path that I was looking for and that I wanted to walk on.

But how to do it?

And one day, my path crosses with that of Michel Houttekens. It is the start of the nineties. Michel, who would become my reiki master, had been taught by Mme Takata.

I want to participate in one of his reiki formations. I call to register … but unfortunately it is too late, the workshop is already full. I hang up, feeling a bit disappointed, but not for long. My phone rings and it is Michel Houttekens, who calls me back: "There is a space for you." And just like that, I end up in Angers to start my initiation to reiki. At the start, I am wondering where I have landed. Michel must have seen my hesitation, when I came in, and invites me to sit beside him. The workshop is in an hotel. Everyone is dressed in white; we are holding hands. I am torn … intrigued … curious.

My curiosity is stronger than my doubts. I decide to keep going and stay. The initiation consists of working on opening chakras by putting your hands on people who are lying down on a table. How am I going to do that? I come closer and I do what I am being told. Try to perceive. I barely put my hands on the individual that is my 'guinea pig' when I feel myself going all over the place. I see colours coming out of people. As I put my hands on him, I see. The body is speaking to me … from the inside! When I put my hands on their body, I have this strange feeling that my hands are going in, inside their body. So, I start telling them what I perceive. The reactions are all different. Some start to cry, others start to get angry and tell me to go away. If they are shaken, I feel the same, shaken, unsettled. I don't understand. Michel reassures me: "You must not say everything." My reading is too intrusive, I see too many things.

Leaving Michel's workshop, I understand that I am in the right place. With this experience, I have the feeling of swimming in magic. I then take the decision: I will commit myself to take the next three years of teaching with him. With each session, I learn, I connect with the fantastic. My knowledge deepens every time. In 1993, I am a reiki practitioner.

The more you feed the light, the more you can help.

I cannot stop seeing the symbols that I felt during the first workshop. *Let it come, you will see later. Don't let the signs that are still mysterious, burden you.* So I let myself be, follow my intuition. I keep going according to the teaching of Mme Takata. My reiki apprenticeship takes five years.

For me, these learning years are pure magic, I discover a universe until then unknown to me, a universe that I could feel but could not put my finger on. With reiki, as it happens, it is through the hands. And very soon, I start to transmit. The most powerful sensation that I have through reiki can be translated with a picture. When I put my hands above someone, to heal, to listen, I feel my hands gliding inside that person. My hands explore and see for me.

I open myself to the invisible world. My master, who initiates me on his land, is a master deeply connected. With him, I feel the world expand. Mantras and meditations are part of my daily routine.

At the end of the nineties, I can no longer stay still. Physically and spiritually, I need to move on. I am coming to the end of my reiki teaching, I am communicating my knowledge to others. Reiki is a pedestal, a very solid base. But it is not enough for me. I wake up during the night. Mantras keep coming to visit, I want to go to India. To explore. I can hear mantras that are pushing me to go further.

One of the foundations of reiki, which also happens to be one of the foundations of shamanism, wants for all things to have a soul. All things! Humans can get in touch with this soul. This communication can bring an energetic healing as well as an open perception of subtle information.

A Journey of Self-discovery

A teacher, a monk, comes close to me. The man puts his hands on my head. At this moment, a powerful emotion goes through me, I start to cry. I cry abundantly, I feel joy in meeting this person and have a profound feeling of knowing him already. He is finally here. I don't know him but strangely we recognise one another and I cry. I wake up, it was a dream. In the morning, when I get up, I tell my husband: "I am going to India."

And just like that, I start my initiation with my Hindu masters. I will be going to India for the next ten years, back and forth. I generally go to India for about a month at a time, visiting ashrams but also meeting with families and women.

I like going above and beyond what I live, this occidental world that keeps complaining. I learn so much, compassion, limitlessness, the power of silence.

An Indian friend teaches me to be limitless. He keeps repeating: "You, you are not scared." Together, we work on my breathing. When I breathe in, I learn to perceive, in full consciousness, the world around me. I can explain it by saying that what I see comes inside me. The picture I see, the vision in front of me: I swallow it. This moment, very powerful, still gives me the shivers today.

It is about working on your breathing through a form of meditation. "You are not scared of falling in the void, as you might be when you are on the edge of a cliff, your feet at the edge of the abyss. You, you are not scared. Feel the vastness, inhale this aspect of the reality." That's what my Indian friend keeps repeating to me. I discover this strength in me, to the point that I find myself breathing in and inhaling the world. I discover this powerful feeling: everything comes inside me. I am now face to face with this vastness, limitless.

Indeed, at a very precise moment when I concentrate on my breathing, on an inhalation, a very strong intoxication envelops my being, creating a vertigo feeling such as I have never encountered before. Everything comes into my little person! I cannot hold onto a scream! The picture (the one I see) submerges me. I learn how to control this breathing, in order to give this vastness.

I do a lot of meditation; I feel totally in my element. The meditation is not a peaceful moment where nothing happens. Meditation allows for the revelation of a different level of consciousness that escapes us. I remember very clearly intense levels of consciousness that I touched while meditating. For example, one day where I am in front of a giant buddha. I am doing my meditation, it is my world, my place. A strange phenomenon is happening ...

I am meditating, facing this buddha, a few metres high. I feel a strong inner peace, supported by the mantras that the monks are repeating. Suddenly I feel a presence, right beside me. Unsettled, I open my eyes: it is me! Immediately my heart starts racing, I am scared. I see myself! There, meditating! That's when I developed a better understanding of the work the monks were doing, to be able to go out of their body and go somewhere else. Later, I would go through a similar experience but in a different form. I would feel my entire body "disintegrating", but I will come back to that later.

These experiences, unexplained and inexplicable, were born from a lot of time of contemplation and meditation.

In India, I had the opportunity to receive the teaching of Sathya Sai Baba, a master able to materialise anything. Sathya Bai Baba is becoming more and more well known, and more and more controversial. (I would later find out that some people abused his fame to become ... profiteers.) A very contested person, but I have seen him.

During one of his teachings in India, in which I was participating, I asked for a very specific necklace. We cannot quite believe it, but we saw it. I am with a friend, I imagine this necklace, creating it in my own mind. To be more specific, I think of a necklace with very specific ornaments and designs. We go to the workshop. During the ceremony, to my astonishment, he takes out a necklace, exactly the one I imagined earlier. To each of us to accept or not this spontaneous creation. But for me, I saw my thought becoming reality. Of course, it was a bit of a shock, but I did not stay fixed on this "creation", I carried on my journey with Sai Baba.

In Kerala, South India, with the monks, I do several journeys of meditations where we share everything. The daily chores are shared between everyone.

My duty one day was to arrange the cushions for the persons meditating. An anecdote comes back to me. We are in the ashram. Now is the time for meditation. As we come out of our rooms, I notice the master leaving his room. I look at him and I hear a voice: *I am going to fall, but it is OK*. I am baffled and tell my friend, Beatrice, who is standing next to me, what I have just heard. We head to the ceremony. We all get ready and forget about the excitement we just had outside. We are all meditating when ... a noise. The master has fallen. General worry seizes the room. I keep telling people not to worry, that everything is OK (don't tell them that I know it because I heard it). The master is OK, the ceremony carries on.

During this period, I was in such a state of mind that people could send me messages. In other words, I could read in people thoughts, a very exciting connection.

Less spectacular, no doubt, but still very powerful teaching, I learn compassion. Compassion that I can feel towards myself first.

India 2006, here is what I wrote:

I am coming out of the ashram, I am crying, I am crying out of anger, out of sadness, out of discouragement, out of ignorance, I am crying out of gratitude, I am crying out of illusion, I want to open my eyes, I want to see further, and I want my illusion to fall. I want to be responsible and realise all my choices.

I say stop! Stop to all the shambles in my head, I want to find inner peace between the child in me and the adult in me.

Life taught me that we don't save people from themselves ...

We can love them, accompany them, support them, encourage them ...

But in reality, each of us saves ourselves. One saves oneself.

The work that I do to find myself, to get closer to myself, asks me for a lot of time.

This introspection is scary, it feels uncomfortable, I know it, but I also know that this a necessity in my everyday life. I don't want to spend my time ... passing myself! I don't want to spend my time avoiding myself, avoiding touching myself, avoiding flirting with myself only because I am not yet capable of loving myself, my whole being.

I don't want to go to others to look for something I can't find within myself.

So can I really love others the way they are, if it does not all start with loving myself first?

This teaching demands of me some work, a lot of work. I comprehend compassion. The first step is about learning to love yourself, love yourself just as you are. Love myself the way I am.

It is not possible to have compassion for others if we are not able to challenge ourselves with compassion. Experience it yourself. Prove yourself. Keep in mind that we are all everything that exists, from our perverse, selfish side to our bright, beautiful side, we are everything. I learn to love everything that is a part of myself. With the help of the monk from Kerala, I manage to accomplish this work.

In one of the ashrams, I develop my learning of the mantras, learn to know them better. I meditate surrounded by their sounds and the meaning of their words. When the master sings, I enter a state of elevation! The chants, the mantras fill me up like a vase. My legs, my stomach, my body fill themselves. I am full of these chants. My entire being imbibes, like the earth waiting for the rain.

In India, I have the need to rejuvenate, I do different retreats, fasting, healing, silence.

And always, when I sing the mantras, I feel the divine going through me. So, one day, I feel like an envelope melting over me; compassion so intense that it floods me. I actually become compassion. When I openly tell my master, he only has one explanation: I have integrated the chants of compassion, the mantras of compassion. "The intention that you hold, your body resonates it!"

It is only there, in India, that I feel this strength; in France it feels different. Our occidental world, closed in by its materialistic weight, cannot perceive the divine subtle incarnation of the mantras.

Another beautiful thing I learn in India, I owe to my friend Bilal. He brings me to experience silence. A total silence. The one that opens infinite and unsuspected connection. We forget what silence is. Yet it is a wonderful 'place' where we can connect with ourselves, where we can find peace. Silence can be a marvellous friend, it can guide you to a place where it does not matter what happens, you will find inner peace.

Thanks to Bilal, I learn to exceed the notion of time. When Bilal talks about it, I am not sure I understand what he means. So to be able to understand, nothing better than a little practical exercise. Bilal takes me to a little hut. For a few days, locked in the dark, I sit. That simple. In total darkness. The only distraction is the bowl of rice that someone gives me every now and then. Perhaps during the night, because even during those times, when the door opens, it is dark outside. I stay there for a few days. Sure enough, I lose all notion of time, locked up with myself.

In that space where time fades away, demons emerge, demons that can bring you to the verge of madness. The Indians call them dragons. These dragons, that we all have deep inside of our being, appear at times where we are not expecting them, in the dark of the hut, in the dark of our consciousness. As things progress, as time passes, the notion of time fades away. And only then our being can touch the essential.

To rediscover the essential 'me'. During this meditation, the demons, the black things, exist by the simple fact that each of us makes them exist. Theses demons end up by vanishing. When my friend Bilal felt that I had taken the step, that I had rediscovered my essential me, he then opened the door. And little by little I rediscover the light. After finding it deep within, I can finally go back to the light, the daylight. I leave my hut.

In this little hut, I discovered the power of the silence. Since then, silence has become my best friend. When I leave the hut, I am not the same person.

After all my encounters, I end up in a village of fishermen. I stay with the women, I share their daily lives, chores. I might not speak their language, but I still communicate with them, by gestures, by eye contact, and of course with the spirit. At times, their language becomes transparent, it flows through me. I understand, I hear words, incomprehensible to my own language, but I understand, and we are communicating.

In India, everything is simple. Indians are often very simple people, amongst whom we can find great masters, with a great and unique generosity. These people have the greatest richness.

When the fishermen leave, we sing for them to bring fish back. Once they are back with the fish, the sharing is very simple. First, they do not fish more than they need, and when they are back each man goes home with what they need, and whatever is left, the owner of the boat takes. So the owner is the last to get served.

With the Indian women, we collect fruit that is then sold at the market. Between us, there is never real anger, even though there are disagreements. But no black, evil, destructive anger. Among them, I discover a simple life. I feel, deep inside my being, a great satisfaction.

The Indians listen a lot to their elderly (they actually live with their family). They listen to their teachings, take them into consideration ... or not. They wear a lot of colours, put a lot of joy in their life.

I learn to do everything with great simplicity, I remember the colours, the music, the smells. All our senses are in the here and now.

They are in the vibration of life, they are in the movement of life, following what is here. They know how to live in the present.

"Sort out your thoughts," Bilal keeps repeating.

I go to India for about ten years, then I take a different group with me. I want to teach them the evanescence, the detachment. For example, by living with the indigent on the streets. A very tough lesson, for us, children of rich countries. During one of those trips, one of my participants is in a wheelchair. He needed help for the most basic daily movements. In one of the ashrams, he has a revelation about the accident that put him in the wheelchair. The work he does on himself, undeniably, helps him to accept his situation. So much so that he eventually gets out of his wheelchair and start walking with crutches.

A few years later, when our path crosses again by 'coincidence', I find out he now plays the piano. This journey in India opened his conscious to a new path. I was only there to accompany him; he did all the work.

That's how I work.

Live Fully the Magnificent Colour of Your Soul

I am walking, in a very large forest, with a group of people. We are clearly moving forward to save souls, it is our goal, our mission. I am with a huge group; I feel a lot of people around me, who are accompanying me. The lost souls that are waiting for us came out of their bodies; we must save them. Time is important. Quick.

We are walking, we are walking. I am with a multitude, but I also have consciousness that among us is a shaman. Maybe within the group, maybe on the way. I have no idea where, but I know a shaman is here. We finally reach a cliff edge. I lean forward to see what is below. At the bottom of the cliff, I see a group of people together around a fire, but what I see scares me. I distinguish their souls, out of their bodies; the souls are floating, escaped from their bodies. I am immediately very worried. I can hear myself say: *But we will never make it on time to bring the souls back into their bodies!* I feel that we have to act quickly before something bad happens. At this precise moment, I hear a voice beside me. This voice says: *You can transform yourself … you can put all the lost souls back into their bodies.* Stunned, I look at this person who is speaking to me. I understand it is the shaman I felt before on the way. I understand. I transform myself into an eagle. Without thinking, without preamble, I fly towards the souls and ask them to return to their bodies immediately. Everything happens very quickly. I go back onto the cliff edge … and I wake up.

Sitting on the bed, still feeling emotional, I feel my husband Bruno staring at me. "Are you OK? What just happened?"

I can only answer: "I don't know …" and without taking the time to reassemble my thoughts, I add: "I think I need to go to Peru. I just met a person who is encouraging me to go to Peru."

During this period, I meet up with a friend who tells me about a wonderful person that he met: a woman shaman who gives ayahuasca. He describes the woman. We are talking about the same person, the shaman in my dream and the woman he met. When he shows me a photo, I am hardly surprised to see the woman in my dream, the one who said: *You can transform yourself.* Emma will teach me a lot (I will come back to our meeting in more detail later).

Yes, I have made my decision. I am going to Peru. However, I need money to get there. I have started working as a reiki therapist, I get some money every now and then, but that's about it. One morning, I receive a cheque from a client. I look at it twice. This particular client had a spectacular healing. It is the start of the euro and I ask myself if maybe she has made a mistake; maybe by error she added a zero to the amount? I call her straight away. "No, no, Francoise, if I give you this amount, it is only because it corresponds to the amount I wish to give you." It is the exact amount I need to fly to South America.

So here we go, direction Peru. A very long trip. I go without any fixed plan, I look. First, I must find a cheap hotel in Lima before flying to Pucallpa. Once there, I am struck by the misery, the dirt that surrounds me, the waste floating on the river. It is a fishermen's village; their huts are made of corrugated metal. Straight away, I start looking for someone who can bring me closer to my dream vision, someone who will help me save souls. I stroll on the verge of the river near the pirogues, walking amongst the plastic bags. I end up coming across this man, who says to whoever wants to hear: "Shaman, shaman." Without a second thought, I say: "Yes, let's go!"

I have great determination, alone but determined. OK, let's do this.

This is my first journey to Peru; I will go on another seven occasions.

Here I am, on my way to the depth of the Amazon, on a nineteen-hour pirogue journey. Everything happens without problem, apart from that night, when the pirogues are stuck on a sandbank. We must come off it and push. The guide keeps looking at the water around us. So much so that I end up asking him what he is looking for in the water at night-time. When I understand that he fears the presence of crocodiles, I, without wasting a second, get back in the pirogue. We then continue our journey.

The sunrise is stunning, the lights, the colours, the birdsong. I am in another world, amazed by what I see, without asking myself what I am doing here. I am astounded by this journey, in the deepest part of this immense forest. I will stay there for three weeks.

In the morning, I open my eyes, I see these huge trees, the river, the animals. Thank you, life, for giving me this opportunity, this journey. I feel as though I am in the right place. I have the same feeling I had when I was in India, when I came off the plane and I was submerged by the powerful sensation: I am coming home. This is where I belong. And I cried. As in India, so in the Amazon.

After all these hours on the pirogue, we approach a small village in the middle of the forest. While we are disembarking, a man welcomes me to the village and says: "I have been waiting for you." I know he is the man I came looking for; he is a shaman.

As soon as I see him, I know. He wears an Antar T-shirt and has a splendid smile. I recognise him from his smile. He fits right in with the energy in my vision with the shaman, my dream, the race to save the lost souls. On entering the village, I am welcomed by a swarm of children. They run towards me to touch me. And I feel as if I need to be pinched; I find myself in such a surreal situation, face to face with this Shipibo Indian, with an Antar T-shirt and these children fluttering around me. They are here to see this foreigner. All the way through my stay, I never fail to be stunned by the freedom that these children have. They take charge of themselves, without adult supervision, and there are no accidents.

The shaman and I, of course, don't speak the same language. He speaks Shipibo. Yet, we understand each other. I have no idea how to explain it other than that our understanding goes through our thoughts; for me there is no verbal understanding. We talk to each other without needing words. I see him smile, I interpret his expressions, we get on really well. So, I stay three weeks with him. We are fasting, and this man tells me: "You are a shaman." I disapprove, but for him, it is very clear that I have a connection with the spirits, with the invisible world. For me, it is their tradition and not mine, so I keep disagreeing. Yet, I feel as though I need to be here. With the shaman, I do a lot of things. I learn about the plant.

I learn to connect with nature, with the animals. More than ever, immersed in the heart of the forest, I feel that we are part of a big everything. I am the tree, I am the bird. I belong to the universe.

If You Have Doubts, Remember Why You Started …

I am going to meet the plant with the help of my shaman guide. The plant has been described as extraordinary. So, one night, the shaman gives me the 'aya', the teaching plant. Night is falling and he gives me a big glass of a thick concoction. I drink it and he indicates that I need to sit further away. I move back and wait.

I am sitting and nothing happens. The shaman starts singing. I am waiting. Nothing that I was told about happens, no colour, no sensation. Nothing …

So, a bit annoyed, I think very loud (for his attention): *if that's what shamanism is, well you are a very small shaman. If you have other things to show me …*

I did not have the time to finish my sentence that a ball of fire is racing towards me. It is coming from this 'small' shaman. And I feel like I am exploding. My arms, my legs, my head, my body scattering in all directions, like a strike when you play bowling, except that the pins are my members. While I am trying to get myself together, I can hear him laugh.

And he starts to sing, like he is never going to stop.

I am scattered. I am being sick. One thing seems to be more important right now: I need to gather myself. In my head, I

hear: *Help!* My body has exploded. For most of the night, I try to reassemble it. I keep repeating to myself: I must put it back together. I listen to the chants, and little by little I relax. The panic that I felt starts to disappear. I can go to sleep. During the subsequent days, we carry on but with more kindness.

The shaman teaches me how to be more centred with myself, to stay inside of myself, in order to see what's beyond, to see what we don't normally see. I work in a way that I can see inside me what is invisible. I discover with insight my feelings, the angers and the joys. The plant allows me to discover this universe, I am experiencing it.

I am becoming the plant.

My key word, my mantra becomes: no resistance. From the moment I take these words for myself, my journey happens without any pain. The medicinal plant, I give it my full trust, and in return, it gives me the opportunity to meet with the depth of my being. I don't know what I am going to live, I don't know where life is going to take me, but I feel it is important for me to meet grandmother plant. According to Shipibo's belief, I am meeting down with the roots of the earth. I will only understand it afterwards. By taking the plant, I answer a very powerful call. Later, I will clearly perceive that this journey, to the hollow of my being, brings me back to the root of the earth, the encounter with wisdom. By following the call, I take consciousness that I have a great listening skill. I discover myself. By listening to myself, I can now listen to others.

During this initial journey, I am visited. By a jaguar.

I am sitting and crouching; beside me the shaman sings.

Suddenly I see my mouth opening widely; while still asking myself how I can open my mouth in such a way, beyond what is reasonable, I feel the jaguar entering. A power enters me. At that moment, I don't feel alone, but inhabited by a magnificent energy.

With the plant, under the directive, the intuition of the shaman, I learn to connect with all the spirits of nature. I learn to respect nature even more, respect the plant, the animals, the living world.

To respect *my* world.

I will do a few journeys with the Shipibo. The powerful work with the plant is not the only thing I do. With the Shipibo, I also learn about vision quests. I will know some beautiful states of consciousness.

Vision quest allows one to come into a modified state of mind and brings you to see beyond yourself.

In small group, we go into the forest. After a little while, the shaman stops in a specific place that he picked. I know that I have to draw a circle on the floor. This circle will become my 'home' for the next four days, without food, without anything. I stay inside this circle in the heart of the forest, alone.

There is a specific ritual that prepares you for this quest, particularly with bags of tobacco. The preparations consist of putting tobacco in little bags, while placing a particular intention for a person, which corresponds to *mitakuye oyasin,* 'you are another me'. *Mitakuye oyasin* means 'to all my parented (the other me)'. And it claims that everything is linked, that we are interdependent, all living beings, Mother Nature. So, I had prepared a few bags, full of intentions according to my relationships.

From that moment, I come into silence. I am in my circle, I put my body into a sleep mode. I start my fasting, only drinking water. And I go through so many states of mind. Why am I here? Questions keep coming. The mind starts going at full speed, loads of images from my past start coming back up.

Time passes. I enter into a second state of mind. All around me, in the vegetation surrounding me, I hear a noise … some sort of beastie. My conscious focuses on this animal, as if I can hear this animal's spirit. I can talk to it! Then arrives, even bigger and more majestic, another animal. I couldn't identify it, but we exchange something. Don't ask me how, but we are in communication. On its command, my spirit follows this animal. Without being able to see it, I feel that it is big and moves with grace. It guides me to the entrance of a cave. Not without apprehension, I enter, and I start to discern, sitting on the floor, a person. Some objects are lying in front of her. I go and sit in front of her. My eyes are slowly getting used to the darkness.

This person in front of me starts moving her lips, as if she is trying to say something. I say: "I cannot hear what you are saying. I can tell you are speaking, but I cannot hear anything." She is a woman with long, white hair; not an American Indian even though she looks like one. Above all, I notice that she is an old woman. She gives me a glass, filled with liquid, that I drink. This time, I can hear her speak but I don't understand her words. The cave is humid, the atmosphere is strange. This woman gives me another glass. I drink. She is now staring at me; I can feel she is taking her time to articulate in order to be heard. She looks deep into my eyes and speaks out softly: "I am you." My spirit gets carried away; everything explodes in my head. I start crying, I start laughing, I go through all sorts of different states, emotions.

I come back to my one-metre-diameter circle. Whatever happens, I must stay here. I must stay with myself.

I will relive this experience later in France; every time I see or feel powerful things that allow me to come into communication. Refocus. It is as if Earth was giving me her energy so I can feed from it. So, I thank it and I give her back this energy. With the vision quests, I am in total communication with Earth, an exchange of energy. A perfect communication. I see trees everywhere, speaking. I am then able to enter into complete vibration with all my surroundings.

The shaman can go beyond appearances; I simply developed this capacity that we all have. A teaching of primary and fundamental values is what I learn from my time with the Shipibo. Today, I can say that the more I connect myself with Earth (the wind, the trees ... all these spirits, because everything is spirit), the more I feel alive!

I also participated in rituals that can be frightening. During one of those rituals, I found myself buried. Alive, soil covers my body; with only a straw to breathe in between my lips, eyes covered with a blindfold, I can hear everything, times ten. My heart! And especially, I can hear the noise that the soil makes as it falls covering my body. I have the sensation that Earth is swallowing me. I can see myself dying. I feel the soil coming inside me. I am torn between being conscious of being alive and having a feeling of dying. The fear of dying is approaching, powerful, but I feel alive, and I have trust. Earth is enveloping me but paradoxically I feel alive. I die from what I am. I pursue my quest.

After this experience, I learn to relativise: I am alive! What is my real need?

I am at the heart of the forest. In order to eat, I grill fresh fish. I go and pick a pineapple. What is my real need? I exchange, share with the women daily, I play with the kids, and there is always time for a nap. Even if our ways of communication are limited, I can still exchange with people, mainly through gestures. I have an authentic relationship with the shaman's wife who offers me her traditional costume. I can be part of a celebration between villages, where the young people meet up in preparation for getting married. I am thankful for sharing their lives. I love their songs, including their scared songs, their healing songs. I learn to perceive the colours of the songs! During a healing song, I see the sound going into the person. The shaman works with a particular intention. He does not offer these songs to everybody.

With the plant, I discovered that every word has a vibration. And it is even more obvious through songs. The first time I saw the vibration of the word 'love', I was shocked! A shape with some translucid, glutinous strings! It was in fact a representation of all the beliefs that people project onto the word love. This is what I saw, a thing that I can only describe as slimy, tangled up, stuck in all the projections that people have. Before, I never considered that word existed. I am Francoise and that's it. Words, for me, were only a point of reference, very limited. But suddenly I had the vision of the word love … a repelling and hideous heap surrounding it, making it impossible to exist. All our projections, our beliefs, binding to the original word. Love was engulfed by all our fears, our desires, our expectations.

But for me, in order to exist, a word needs to be pure. With the word's vibration, I must commit myself to purity in order to use this or that word.

The plant gives all the keys.

During another journey, a night where I am with the Shipibo, I dream of a tarantula. The tarantula is making its web, I watch it weaving life's colour. In my dream, the result is beautiful, this spider is weaving the strings of life. The tarantula is telling me about myself, with its web, (even though, in reality, a tarantula does not weave a web, but instead digs a nest). It symbolises who I am, on the lookout for my emotions. It is showing me the colours of life through the lines in its web. I keep this impression of a beautiful set.

Once the morning comes, we start tidying up our sleeping area. I am with two friends, Magali and Emma. I am telling them all about my strange dream; all night I had a feeling of being in communication with a tarantula, that the spider was speaking to me through its weaving. We are all chatting while tidying up. Magali lifts up my pillow and can't help but jump back! Under my pillow there is a tarantula. Emma says that it is without a doubt a sign. I am not scared. I slept all night with a tarantula.

It is not scared of you, because you, you are not scared of it.

The shaman taught me to not exhale fear, like that day we were walking in the forest. We are going further and further in this botanic maze, until the shaman decides we can sit on the floor. In this position, I listen to the forest. Unexpectedly, I hear, coming from behind me, the roar of a jaguar. The shaman makes me understand: trust, don't give out the fear emotion. Easy to say, but you know there is a huge wild cat walking behind you … I can feel fear rising up. I listen to his guidance. My reaction is to connect with the forest, enter in communication with the trees, the plants, the air, the water. I manage to connect myself with this thrilling world. And everything changes. The jaguar keeps on its path, and we then continue on our journey. I understand that everything is simple. The basis of all teaching, knowledge is there, we don't need high technology to connect to things, to each other, everything is here. We just need to listen.

With the Shipibo, we do not eat meat every day. Eating meat demands a particular ritual. The Shipibo ask Mother Nature. When they decide to kill a chicken, it starts with a drum. They start a ritual until one chicken, following the sound of the drum and the chants, comes forward. The chicken is offering itself as a sacrifice. The universe gives this offering to the Shipibo. Our world is the opposite, we have intensive farming where all sense of nature is lost.

All along my different journeys, I learn to communicate with this 'everything', that I can read as if it is visible. I discover that shamanism is very elementary, in the sense that it is in direct connection with nature. Everything is there. It is a way to sign up to the world, to survive. For me, shamanism is the basis of life, we should all learn it.

We are all part of this everything, this living.

Today, I keep defending this notion, in my life as well as during my workshops.

The weather is dull, it is cold, it has been raining. I go outside with the members of my workshop. We are standing on wet grass. I ask each and every one of them to pace the grass barefoot, understand the earth directly. I can feel some hesitation. Take your shoes off if you really want to connect with the earth. I then ask them to stamp their feet until they follow the rhythm of the drum. After a while, by the simple movement of stamping their feet, the participants start to release their tension and apprehensions I can see them cry. One of the women in the group tells me: "I can feel Earth's heartbeat all over my body!" She is agitated. Barefoot to feel!

I need to connect myself.

We very often put complicated words on the word shamanism, but in reality, it is just simple. Shamanism is nothing more than a link with nature, a reading of the world to which we all belong; our world that we must learn to love.

Simplicity is not a Quest

To be simple, modest, to be human is not an equation that rhymes with simplicity, and yet, we all have so much to learn from this concept. Through all my travels, I learnt a lot, but travelling is not essential. Unquestionably, wherever we are, in order to find peace and harmony with this "everything", a talent comes into force (and not a rule, I am not the kind of person to make rules, on the contrary). This talent is to be human, be modest.

Simplicity is not a quest, it is here.

We, well most of us, have lost it; we erased it by competitivity, buried under a mountain of technology. Irony, under the pretext of a simplified life, this technology, that we do qualify as high, this tool, so precious in our eyes, actually cut us off from simplicity. Because this high tech disengages us from our inner senses.

Sitting on the top of a mountain, I breathe in the limitlessness. I receive a magistral life lesson. What is simpler? What is richer?

At home, I listen to the surrounding that speaks to me. I feed myself from what surrounds me, and I am thankful. To have a shelter and listen to the sound of the storm on the roof.

We must find this silence deep inside ourselves, by starting to be thankful for what we are living, to be happy with what we have. Only then, we notice that we don't need anything. At the time of writing, this spring 2020, I am in lockdown. The lockdown, imposed by the Covid19 pandemic, brings us back to the essential.

Locked in my house, I take full advantage of doing nothing. I observe, I listen. The sun, the birds … the race against time seems to be over. I find the same satisfaction I had in India, in South America, in Asia. I feel joy, because something vibrates inside, a joy, a surrounding.

I learn to feed this joy.

Inspiring Relationships
Emma, I, Us

Amongst the beautiful meetings I encounter in my life, there is this woman.

At the start of the year 2000, I meet Emma. She is one of the people who counts in a lifetime. She became a friend. And now she is gone. Once more, it all started in a dream. This founding dream, where I walk to save souls, this dream where a woman tells me: "You can transform yourself." This woman is Emma.

So, one night I dream about the shaman woman. When I wake up, I have a strong feeling to see her in front of me. She is here! As I mentioned previously, a little while after this dream, a friend visits me and tells me about this wonderful woman he met up with recently. And she also gives 'the plant'. She organises seminars, workshops in Belgium and Switzerland. When he shows me a photo, I recognise her straight away. She is definitely the woman in my dream. So, on the same day, I decide to go and visit her. She lives in the south of France. A few hundreds of kilometres later, I find myself knocking on her door, even though I was told: "Emma, you cannot just meet her like that!"

I knock. Emma opens the door, and she tells me: "I have been waiting for you."

That night, where we meet for the first time, we talk like old friends. Without a doubt, we know, we know each other. This conversation, talking about this and that, will stay with me. I stay for a few days, and even join her at one of her ceremonies. A few weeks later, I fly to Peru.

Emma is at the origin of one of my life's paths.

With Emma, all the way through our conversation, I learn. I discover that she is a person with a real connection with the universe. She communicates with all the spirits, and she does it with ease, with so much love that it becomes palpable. Emma also has this unique ability to be able to play different roles, in her life as well as during the seminars. Very quickly, she becomes intangible. She is feared when she becomes angry; however a few words are enough to make her come out of the role she is playing. She is a very talented actress; she plays to show the palette of human emotions. And she is very good at it!

Emma teaches me a lot. Non-stop and always with fun, she guides me.

One evening, she offers me a gift. We are in Morocco; it has been a very hot day and the temperature is cooling down. We are making the most of the weather and settle ourselves on a rooftop. Upon her request, we sit down facing each other.

"Now, you are going to look at my inside book." To my surprise, I discover that it is possible to read a person … like 'an open book'! With Emma, who opens herself, I find out that I can, without pretence, read people's souls. In total trust, Emma offers me this gift. I can see inside, far beyond the physical aspect. This discovery baffles me, and it will in the future open a lot of doors.

Thereafter, we organise seminars together, gathering up to a hundred and fifty people. Emma gives us a basic teaching, to take roots with Earth. To make links. Everything I teach today comes from that.

I discover Emma as my soul mate. She emanates real love. We organise seminars, one right after the other, in the south of France, in Belgium and in Switzerland. In everyday life, Emma is whole-heartedly the person she plays. I reconnect with the magical side of existence.

As things progress, during our travels and seminars, a small group of people starts forming. A hard core of followers, who fall into adulation.

One night in Belgium, as per our custom, we find a quiet time to chat. That night, we talk, and talk, and talk. She confides in me that she is tired of her life, she wishes for other things. During our conversation, I clearly see on her wheel of life, a black dot. The seminar ends. I decide to stay in Belgium, she goes to Switzerland.

On the way, Emma dies in a motorbike accident. When I find out, I sincerely think, her soul decided to leave her body. If Emma, so powerful and loved, is gone, she, without a doubt, decided so.

Following her disappearance, I have a lot of dreams, with one very precise. I am walking on a path, and I feel that I have gone too far. Right at this moment, I hear a familiar voice that says to me: "What are you doing here?" It is Emma. "You should not be that far. Come, we will sit down." Emma, sitting on a rock, starts a long conversation. She is still teaching me.

When I wake up, I remember this dream, but unfortunately, I cannot remember Emma's words. However, during my everyday life, I can feel her presence. I have the certainty she is here, tickling my thoughts.

Even today, I believe she is always present, in her own way.

The Road to Creation

Maybe it is due to extreme luck that I met him? I am in Brussels, participating in one of his conferences. I am listening to Olivier Masselot. His chosen field is quantic energy, and the words he is saying really do move me. Deeply.

Olivier is putting what I am living into words. At the end of his conference, I want to speak with him; but so many people are trying to do the same that I give up, saying to myself that if one day I succeed, it will happen when it is supposed to happen. I go home feeling touched by all the words he pronounces. His words have a true echo deep inside me.

A little while later, I go to a seminar in the south of France, near Montpellier. I am not very far from Hameau de l'étoile, a place I am already familiar with. I have a look at the programme they offer. One of Olivier Masselot's seminars is starting very soon. I am with a friend; we enquire about the seminar: fully booked! Not feeling disheartened, I decide to go there. But at reception, I get the same answer: it is fully booked. I ask the receptionist if they have any accommodation available as I would love to spend some time in this peaceful place. There are only two spaces left in a little cabin, not the most comfortable place, but better than nothing. As I am discussing the arrangement with the receptionist, Olivier Masselot enters. He asks what I am looking for. I explain why I am here, and he answers: "For you, there is a space, you can register for the seminar."

Most of the participants are psychologists, psychiatrists and specialists in neurosciences. While on this seminar, I discover a new thing. I understand that within me, there is another space than the one often portrayed. I have a sort of virgin space. Where most people have old memories, I have no souvenirs, not even a trace of memories.

I then make the following assumption: I am anchored so much in the present that I don't obstruct myself with the past. In other words, I don't carry with me ancient stories that could potentially slow me down or even destroy me. I am free of these remnants, and without a doubt, lighter to move forward.

Maybe I am living so much in the present that the rest loses its importance?

Rightly so, during the seminar, Olivier explains that where we put importance is what we see. In other words, if we don't put importance on such and such a thing, we won't see it. These words ring in me with a powerful force.

Following this seminar, I follow Olivier for about two years. I register for his seminars, I follow him on visioconferences. I learn more and more (Oliver speaks about 'transurfing'). At least, I learn to put words where I never thought possible. Very quickly, with Olivier, I have full trust. He lets me coach various groups, I work on visioconference and I start to spread what he has taught me.

What I keep from his teaching is the possibility to put words on what I see and feel. Olivier talks about quantic energy. I can link this energy with my vision of the world.

In a general way, I discover that I have (it seems to me) a vision that is bigger and, at the same time, very selective and very precise. Some talk about eagle vision.

From this observation, the field of the possible opens up. For me, all the elements are present. I can see beyond the physical body. By linking the neuroscience and quantic energy, I can explain what I distinguish a lot better.

The easier way to describe my understanding of the world is that I see strings; and these strings weave the material world. When there is an anomaly, I can see strings that are frayed or even broken. Thanks to this vision, it is possible to intervene. I can sort of mend or even tune them.

This work with Olivier allowed me to deepen my vision, to give it life. Today, when I talk about vibration, I talk as one informed, like a true learning of feelings with my sense sharpened.

My teaching did not come from one day to the next. It depends upon the chances that life offers you, and the meetings that weave from it. I learn as much through my meetings as from my life on a daily basis. Each meeting is important, and some leave a permanent print.

Poland, Here and Now
Say Yes to Life

I found myself teaching in Poland by 'coincidence'. But maybe it was not a coincidence after all? Is there not a saying: coincidence is a plan in disguise? A friend calls me to tell me about his friend who is suffering greatly …

But let's rewind.

At the end of 2014, start of 2015, I feel the need to, how to say it, put myself on standby mode. I go into a state of introspection. I have this urge to be on standby from everything, even food. So, I stay at home, reclusive, in a quiet room, and I meditate. I really need it. It is a very powerful call from within. So, I enter this introspection state without knowing where it is going to take me.

What feeds me today? What am I doing here? These questions present themselves, throbbing, digging their furrows. In order to hear my guides, I keep meditating. And I hear voices saying:

Learn to say yes to life!

Learn to say yes to everything coming your way and pay special attention to what happens when you do say yes. Listen to yourself, what is moving (or not!) from within. Ah? I am baffled but I listen to my guides. Say yes. And during this questioning, I spend time observing the reasons why I was saying no before. I learn.

So, in February 2015, a friend calls. It is important, he explains. A woman who has a wellbeing centre is sick. Seriously sick. Doctors do not know what else to do for her, so this friend thought of me. He calls on me to go and see her, she is in Poland.

The first thing that comes to my head: *Poland, in February! But I am going to freeze to death!* This thought has barely entered my mind, when at the same time, I hear: *Say yes to life! Remember what you said.* This voice that I heard before keeps on at me.

Let the unknown come to you, you are opening a new door.

However, I still hear my mind, that noisy ego shouting at me that I am wasting my time. *Stop!* I listen, I enter a state to listen to what is happening within.

I say yes!

And here we go! I find myself on the next flight for Warsaw. Once there, yes, it is freezing. But it is not the end of my journey, the centre is not near the airport. I still have five hours in a car to get there, to arrive in this … wonderful place. TU I Teraz (Nowe Kawkowo) centre is located within a forest, no less than forty hectares of beautiful forest. Everything is white. The house that is waiting for me is a huge and gorgeous building with a wooden balconet, beautifully sculpted. I have a feeling of finding myself in a fairy world, the smoke is coming out of the chimney, water is running outside. This setting fills me with delight.

But I am not here as a tourist, even if I hear a voice whispering: *Woah, it does exist!* I go and see this woman, Maja. For a week, I accompany her on the difficult path she is going through. We talk, a lot. And I give her treatments at the same time. A translator is by our side; she often makes me repeat what I have to say, I repeat. After a week, I go back to France.

Once I am back home, I get a call. "Maja is healed, she is doing well. She understood what you told her." Then this person keeps the conversation going with this question, that still resonates in my ears: "Do you want to do seminars, here in Poland?"

Yes to life.

Oh Present!

Who is Francoise? A French granny; my long spiritual quest brings me back to my own home where I finally learn to be quiet and listen. A huge thank you and welcome! Life is incredible! Life is a journey we all embark upon, all together, full of mysteries, adventures, discoveries …

My experiences, the meetings I made allowed me to be who I am now. I have a rich life, with more than twenty-five years of experience. I worked in Peru with shamans in the Amazon forest, in India and in Nepal with spiritual guides and with quantic energy, with the law of attraction, in Morocco with the Gnawas women and their trance.

It is through all these encounters that my path was drawn.

I organise seminars in France, in Belgium, in England, in Scotland, in Poland, in Egypt, in Morocco, in India. From all my teachings, I keep the concept to include everything in my life, that all spiritual elevation must be served daily. I have learnt that in time of transformation, all the energy is here, available to all.

I understood that rituals are important to keep contact with our spiritual being.

I understood that each path of life is sacred and that everything starts from our own self.

I am committed to transmit through the heart, because I deeply believe that awareness will change the world, allowing for peace, to offer respect and kindness.

At Maja's request (and despite my resistance) I write this text to introduce myself. Maja, as a director of Tu I Teraz centre (centre aimed at personal and spiritual development here and now), wishes that I reveal what I want to do during the seminars.

I started my first seminars with ten to fifteen persons; today we have on average forty to sixty participants, sometimes reaching up to a hundred. Maja asked me to define my seminars, give a theme with clear explanations of what is going to happen. Only this is not how I work. I can give a general theme, but I don't have a programme. Femininity, man, what is femininity? I never establish a programme. I connect with the energy of the group and depending on the people registered, I work.

This is the way I work every time, as surprising as it seems. However, for some people, it is very disturbing. To tell you the truth, I don't know in advance what we are going to do. I simply tell people that we are going to be together. I believe that now Maja is used to it; for others it is very destabilising.

I work with the present.

These words may seem unintelligible for people who are attached to things, to cut and explain the universe, trying to rationalise everything around us. We must let the magic of the present speak. So depending on the people present during my seminars, I adjust my work. The seminar works depending on what sort of energy the group gives off. Entering the unknown can be disturbing, but it is a great lesson to learn to listen to oneself.

At the centre, I improvise each and every time. The only things that I respect are mealtimes, only to respect the people working hard in the kitchen. Apart from that, everything happens like it should be.

Generally, I start with a talking stick; everyone can express themselves if they wish by taking the talking sticks. The speech establishes itself, without cacophony (thanks to my two translators). Sometimes, the vibrations of the words pronounced are so strong that I don't need a translation to understand the meaning.

Learn to feel what you need, in a specific time.

Every time I organise a seminar, I enter a new vibration. I can only explain it by saying that my perceptions are like musical chords. I listen to everything that resonates within each individual. It gives me the ability to read the person like an open book. On the other hand, I am not here to tell them what I see. I am here to bring the person to see what is within. On the condition, of course, that the person is ready to see.

As I repeat it often, it is your story, not mine. You have to learn to see what is happening within. If I smothered my feelings to be like everybody else, then I am surely passing by who I really am.

To bring each and every one to perceive the present to learn more about themselves.

Each Seminar is Different

Here are some examples of seminars that I organise in Poland, where I go on average about ten times a year.

VI Workshop: Life Sharing – shamanic rituals for the Moon, Fire, Earth and Water. Summer solstice with Francoise Rambaud.

We are in a new era, in a new vibration. We build new relationships, with four elements that will create a new meaning on the planet.

We must learn:

nonverbal communication between us and the spiritual world

to direct our energy only to things that matter.

I link this workshop with the following text, written in 2017.

I will be with you to heal what must be healed in your body and your soul. To close the messages and the links, you do not need anymore. To help you be yourself, to develop your full potential, to assimilate your shadows and your deficiencies. I will teach you healing techniques to benefit all the people around you. Together, we can heal ourselves, our close ones, Mother Nature, and our lives. We have the power to change the world. I am here to help you find your Inner Power, your Inner Power Shaman.

Maja, the director of the Polish centre, added the following:

Attention, attention! Francoise has completely changed how the seminar works: she wants us to concentrate on what is really important for us, far from all the materialistic needs. There won't be a fixed fee for the workshops, each offers what he/she thinks is fair. It is an invitation to a grand gesture, to open your heart … but also a challenge to determine and participate with her expenses (flights, translators, other shamans and musicians) and express your gratitude for the teachings, the accompaniments, and the healing received.

In my own words, I explain that to the participants. I give them an envelope. We are at the end of the seminar. This ritual, I wish to transform it. Usually, everyone puts in the envelope the amount of money corresponding to the cost of the seminar. I wish to change this ritual into an abundance ritual. This moment is revealing our relationship between money and our world. In the envelope, you can put whatever you want, whatever pleases you. Instead of asking you to pay me … This gesture, by the intention put in, reverses itself: you are paying yourself. In other words, with the amount of money you are putting in the envelope, you are thanking yourself for your participation.

This money represents what you receive during the seminar, the great feeling that you allowed yourself to feel. You are giving yourself a recompense. So you choose.

And everyone gives money proportional to their income, but with a strong thought about what they learnt.

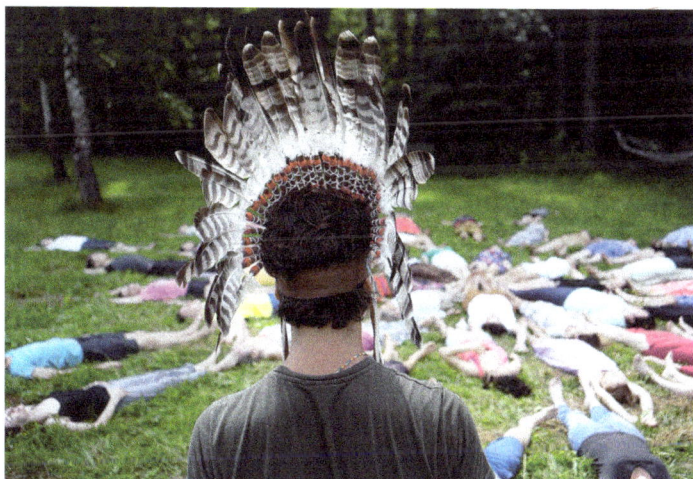

The Doll of Illusions

I am organising a seminar about femininity. A stunning woman is participating. On a different level, she is trying to be a fashionable person, just like the women we see in a magazine. Her appearance is superb. She used (without any doubt) Botox in order to perfect her plastic world. I also find out that she has permanent makeup. I cannot help myself and ask her what she is doing here on a workshop about femininity, and that maybe she made a mistake. A trivial thought springs to mind: *It does exist!* She looks like all these creatures on glossy paper, she looks like nothing.

As the seminar progresses, she reveals herself a bit more. She explains that despite the facts that she showers her conquests with luxurious presents (this woman has a lot of money) such as sports cars, she cannot find a man, a 'real' man, as she calls him. So, I tell her (maybe a bit brutally): "Look at what you have that is real. You cannot find a man, a real one. But look at what you have real in your life? Your bum? Your breasts? Your makeup? Look!"

Observe.

The seminar ends. Time passes, a few months, I think. I am organising another seminar, and a car approaches the centre. A woman gets out of it, along with a man. A real cowboy! I can't help myself from whispering: a cowboy! The woman comes toward me. It is her! I recognise her, despite all the things she has got rid of; no more false nails or other artifice.

We exchange a look and I understand. She tells me her story. She sold everything. Her world as a business woman, she left it all behind. She sold her businesses, her shares. And today she owns a ranch to welcome children in difficult situations.

And she met a man!

This woman found her true self. I brought her to see what she could find beyond her artificial life. She managed to see further than the picture of the woman she wanted to project. What advantages, what disadvantages could she find in a world made with plastic and things? During the seminar, she agreed to show herself, get naked. Literally, she uncovered herself in every sense of the term.

During the seminar, devoted to femininity (we were only women), she, the doll, got undressed, she threw away all her chains. During a very specific moment of the seminar, I proposed, with a lot of kindness, that she get undressed. Others, who wished to do the same, could do the same. We covered her with oil. This ritual brought us back to our bodies, our births, a ritual that brings us close to our uterine passage. I never prepared this ritual, it just happened with the magic of the present. (And of course, with the complicity of my assistants to find oil and everything else rapidly).

I leave my wandering intuition to give birth to creativity.

Never have I tipped into excess. The decision to get naked was done in such kindness. A benevolent and catching energy was surrounding the group. A rebirth happened for a lot of the women there. The example of this doll woman is revealing of this force that we all have: to free the being we have inside us.

To each of us to do the work.

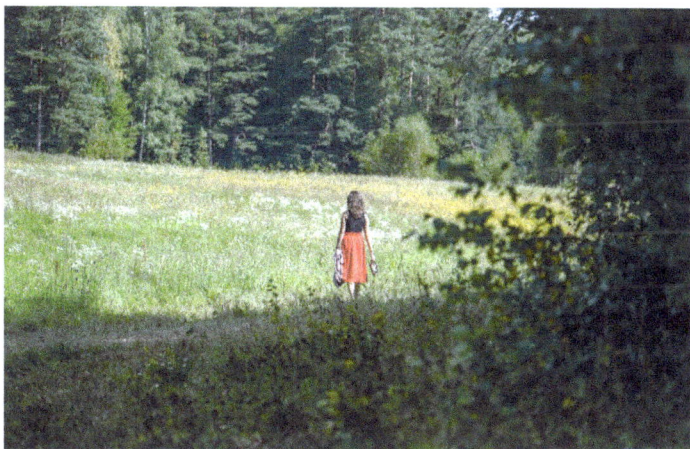

Accepting to go and
Meet Oneself

One day, a woman shows me the undesirable host she is holding on to. I am organising a seminar in the same centre, Tu I Teraz. Very quickly, I notice this person. She is housing a huge anger. OK, but what is behind this anger? We will try to find out.

We are going to play a game, I will suggest one, and you can tell me if that is OK? OK! Let's go!

A young lady finds herself attached to a pillar. And the women around her start to get into the game. They start to insult the 'prisoner', calling her names. Her first reaction is logical, violent; screams of anger gush out. Once this phase is over, we take the prisoner into our arms. We all feel that she is going through a very powerful internal anger. I take her in a warm embrace and slowly, kindly, stroke her face. The contradiction flames up, she is experiencing the fury of the insult and the kindness of the embrace.

Finally, we talk about what she went through. She discovered that she was saying yes to her entourage all the time, submissively. A yes that does not belong to her. She was not listening to herself anymore, she was in the beliefs of her parents, her husband. By letting the anger explode while she was attached, she became conscious of the cage she was trapped in. Immediately, she understood the power of listening. Listening to oneself gives a perfect clairvoyance.

This work is only possible by having a clear perception of the group's energy, without any ulterior motive. I am always conscious of what is going on even if sometimes 'my mouth speaks by itself'. I learn to listen to the group in its diversity and its unity.

Of course, this work is only possible with the particular care of the translators. At the start, I had a translator, but evidently, she did not understand my language, which if I am honest can be difficult to understand for certain ears. Luckily, Maja introduced me to another one. When we first met, we understood each other beyond words. Clearly, we already knew each other.

Today, my work in Poland does not encounter any obstacles, the words flow from French to Polish, we speak the same language.

Other examples of participants spring to mind, but to sum up, I prefer to quote what a Polish woman said about me:

Meeting with an extraordinary person! Some time ago, I met someone on this planet; she had extraordinary capacities and a huge and creative potential. This person actually lives among us, a rather normal life. Her power stays put, even for herself. However, as soon as she starts exploring, and accomplishing her mission in life, with bravery, things start to happen. It is worth meeting this person!

The Man with the Mirror

In the middle of a seminar, a man comes to me. Or rather I ask him to come forward. I noticed his attitude as soon as he arrived at Tu I Teraz. In his body is inscribed the world's weight, he is tired. I ask him to sit in front of me. I put my hand on his chest. The man shudders. Quickly, the tears start to flow. I ask him to look at me to see if he can see himself in my eyes. I tell him that for now, he is not able to see himself. "You do not see who you are. If you really want to see who you are, I can offer you something."

We finally manage to find a mirror, not too big, just what we need, it stands on wooden legs. In order for this man to discover who he is and to learn to see himself, I offer nothing more than a mirror. Using a crafty system, the mirror is attached to the face of our tired man. He will now spend the rest of the seminar looking at his own image. Wherever he goes, he sees himself. At dinner, while eating, during the ceremonies, outside while singing, everywhere he sees himself, he is looking at himself. The only instruction: "Take note of everything you see, everything you feel."

When the end of the seminar is near, he comes to me to summarise his experience. "You know, at the start, when you put your hand on my chest …" deep breath, he keeps going. "I felt something in me exploding, literally."

So I tell him: "I believe that your heart opened up." He carries on, saying that for the past few years, he has had a heart problem, a problem which he takes medication for. Since I put my hand on his chest, he has decided to stop the medication and he has never felt better.

I really believe him because he has clearly changed physically since his arrival at the centre. He stands in a different way, and even though he does not shine, his attitude has changed. He tells me he owns a pharmaceutical company. Upon departure, I can feel that he goes with a new freedom in his hands.

Sometime later, I found out that he left his company for something completely different. He decided to create jewellery, not just any kind, not on a big scale. No, he makes jewellery depending on the person, unique to each individual. He learnt to find himself through making personalised jewellery: how to see oneself.

Love without condition. The big lesson, learn to love oneself, unconditional love.

Going Back to Rituals

When I am in Tu I Teraz, I love practising rituals linked to nature, the elements. It can be very simple, like having a blindfold, and lettting oneself be guided to a place and imagine. Feel and listen to the landscape until you become the landscape and start picturing it ... or things that may require a bigger investment. Regardless of the number of participants, whether it is one or a hundred, it is always the same for me. I vibrate with my group; I am linked with the surrounding energy without looking for understanding.

Recently, I have been working with the water element. The centre is located in a wonderful place, surrounded by nature, and not very far from it there is a lake.

I suggested a purification ritual to all the participants. Each goes into the water. Slowly. There are eighty participants. So eighty people move slowly into the water, step by step. I ask them to keep moving forward, to enter the lake until the water is above their head, until they are completely immersed. And above all, when they start this walk, I ask them urgently to bring all their useless, heavy emotions, the ones that hinder them. While progressing into the lake with their intentions, they ask the lake to clean them, to purify them. The aim is to get rid of all the unnecessary emotions.

I observe and see what is happening. I asked a woman coming out of the lake, happy, to go back. Despite the fact that she is wet, I can see that she is still encumbered. She says that no, she feels fine. So I ask her if she wants me to tell her what I see. As she nods, I say: "I can see all your regrets." Hearing these words, she bursts into tears.

She needs a second time to feel free. And I see a lot of people shining, coming out of the lake.

Another ritual for purification, which is similar, can be done with the fire element. It is possible to allow yourself to be reborn. I work on the idea of 'rebirth'; for example, I ask the participants to lock up in a little bag all the things they do not want to go through. This can be represented by an object, a stick they found in the forest, it can be some tobacco, in short, something that can be burnt but something that is going to carry the intention of the person all day.

Blindfolded, I take them to the forest. In order to move forward, they must trust the voice that guides them. We work in silence, rocked by the silence of the forest. On the way back, aided by my assistants, we form a tunnel. Each participant goes through this tunnel with the intention of rebirth. In the evening, we proceed with the burning of their bags. Each comes to burn their 'burdens' in order to re-emerge, to live something different. We burn these little bags, to free ourselves and simply progress towards our true nature.

During the ceremony, where we sing around the fire, each participant takes turns to throw their burdens. I ask them to observe how the bag falls into the fire, how it burns. When they are ready and the moment comes, I insist the intentions be put into action: thank the part of yourself that you are now letting go of. Of course, everyone says, yes, yes! But when the time comes to do it, to let go of the heavy burden, it is interesting to see how the bags land in the fire. There are as many ways of throwing as there are participants. Some bags fall on the side of the fire, some only half burn, other catch fire very quickly. Others don't seem to be able to throw their bags. So, I go with them and accompany them in their quest for liberation.

I also love using the element of the forest to practise this freedom, this cleansing. I send them on a quest to find an element of the forest. It is all about taking the time to lose oneself in the forest, to let oneself being 'grabbed' by an object. Once the object has been chosen, I ask each and every one of them to "load" this branch, this stick, this leaf, this piece of bark, this plant, this stone … to emotionally load this object with all the intentions of who they want to become. Throughout the seminar, each day, I ask them to honour this chosen object, to show respect and to remember what intention it represents. And each day, to make it more beautiful.

Learn to observe. Be your intentions.

During the summer months, in Poland, thermometers can reach high temperature. I suggest we observe the energy of the wind. And we play. It is very hot. Each enters the game of the wind, we play, we feel, we let ourselves become naïve. It is very hot. Let's ask the wind to cool us down a bit. We start a ritual with that specific intention. Just like magic, the wind cools us down, briefly but so refreshingly.

Like happy kids, we thank the wind, letting joy finds its place.

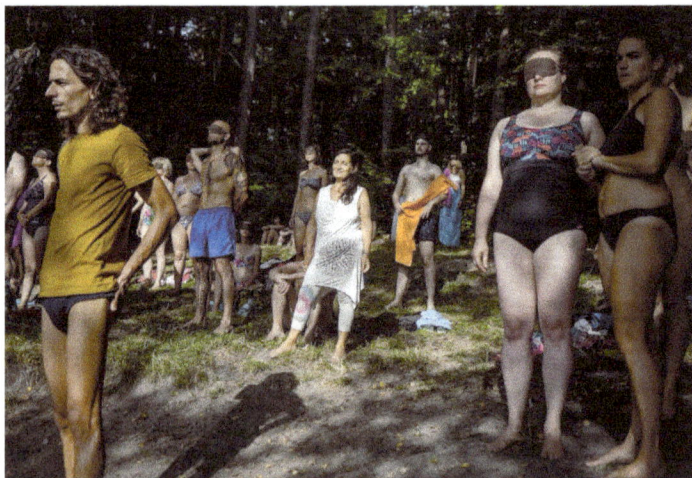

I Feel the Aura

Now more than ever, I have an ultra-fine perception of the universe. The lockdown, linked with the Covid19 outbreak, brought me to experience a period of silence. A period during which I looked inside myself. I really appreciated the silence and the peace.

Following the end of lockdown, I find myself projected into this normal world, and I notice that I am even more sensitive to it all. At different times of my life, I felt things, but more than ever now, I feel more connected with my surroundings.

I develop a capacity of being able to see further. And I don't want to scare you, but I can see more and more people with snakes' heads. As if those persons have lost their true nature. My senses are like receptors … I can be with my feelings, feel the emotions on a pure level. For me, people are like books. I open my senses. I start reading, those around me, what surrounds me.

To the point that I can clearly see the auras, and I have no other words to explain it. Not only do I see the person physically in front of me, but I also see the light surrounding it.

Sitting in the truck, in the passenger seat, beside Bruno, I feel a cold draft along my arm. I move my hand and realise that actually I am touching the outline of Bruno's body. Mechanically, I keep doing my movement. Bruno says: "Thank you, I had a pain in my shoulder, and now it is gone" I am stunned. I express my gratitude towards life.

Since this morning, I cannot stop thinking about my close friends. I keep on with what I am doing; however, my thoughts bring me back to Helene and Amandine. I must call Helene. "Ah! It is you, Francoise. Yes, I am with Amandine. Why are you calling?" We talk, and I explain what I 'see' with her. My explanations allow her to open even more and from that moment on, she can act.

When I am in my house, I love to abandon myself, contemplating nature, particularly the birds. Today, I am sitting quietly in the garden, when I see a buzzard flying by. A thought goes through me. *One day, if you must leave this planet, I will be here for you.* As my day goes on, I forget. With my husband, we are making the most of this beautiful day and we go for a walk. On the way back, as we are nearing the house, we notice on the side of the road, a bird, no doubt hit by a car. We stop and we go to see the bird, this beautiful creature. It is still warm. It is a buzzard; I am holding it in my arms. I feel overwhelmed, on the verge of tears. We cannot leave it on the side of the road. Once we are back home, we celebrate with a funeral ritual for this magnificent bird.

While walking, I notice tree stumps. And rather than tearing off the weeds that surround them, I tell myself: *No, just wait.* Time passes and when I walk past the tree stumps again, the weeds have now opened up and form a beautiful frame to our walk. I hear little voices whispering: *We are the little pixies of the wood.*

And I am careful not to give my energy to people destroying the planet, otherwise I am feeding them.

At this time, if I look at you, I see the other you. Is this an illusion? I see further than your physical appearance, I see the things you don't see. And words are powerless, there are no words to explain what I perceive. I 'see' your inner-me, your inner being. The true you is in front of me. The light, the source that you express is standing there, I see it. And I can feel this purity inside you.

More than ever, I understand humanity. After lockdown, seeing people again affects me. When I go home, I am shivering. I can perceive the entities that inhabit and control them, the fear, the submission. Lockdown allowed me to hear things I did not hear before. Once more, I realise that silence helps with sensitive hearing.

The appearance of the Covid19 pandemic put our fear of dying on the first stage. This fear is multiplied, relayed by all sort of medias as well as ourselves.

Our brain makes molecules following our feelings. If we are happy, the brain makes some molecules, if we are stressed, it makes other molecules, and so forth … depending on our emotions. If we are scared, if we hold onto the fear of death constantly, our brain will start making the necessary molecules constantly. In my opinion, we just need to have a flaw, a crack in our being, for the fear to infiltrate us, and break us, sometimes to the point of destroying us.

In other words, I see this fear like roots. They develop and are capable to slide inside us, especially if we have flaws to grip on even more.

It depends on each of us to stop driving this dominant and dominating fear. Simple things are enough (if only just turning off the tap of news coming in).

For me, silence can be a great source of inspiration. And even more, it becomes a place where I can revitalise, where I know to find the universe's soul. Once I am in complete silence, my perception is more subtle, more clear; I don't enter matter, I am part of it.

Accepting to not Understand Everything

Recently, before going on to one of my seminars in Poland, something happened. A story that I don't understand, and maybe never will.

My daughter, Julie, calls me one night regarding her son. He is thirteen, and not coming out of his room. Julie asks me if I can do something for him. Thirteen years old can be a difficult time. I must say that he has been going through a tough time for a while.

His younger brother, instead of calling him by his name, kept calling him Archie. That lasted for about two or three years. He was quite a withdrawn child, with a lot of anger. Growing up, he was often the subject of bullying. During the lockdown, he found it difficult to stay in touch with his friends. Not long ago, he confided in me that when he feels anger rising to the explosion, deep inside, he has the feeling that it is not him.

Following his mother's phone call, I connect myself to him, I try to get in touch with my grandson. I immediately see … a grey shape. I say to myself that this 'thing' has nothing to do here. I take it off him. The next day, Julie calls me again. "I am not sure what you did, but he is completely transformed. He got up this morning, he is smiling, and he seems to be a lot better."

Excellent! I don't try and understand, the result is here so I am happy. Days pass, and I must go to Poland for my next seminar. Life goes on. Once I arrive, I meet the participants; one by one, they come and say hello. My friend, Philippe, is accompanying me. "Hello," "Hello," they all come to us. Here comes a man, a young man; as he approaches us, Philippe looks at me and says: "Don't you think he looks like your grandson?"

Taken aback, I must admit there is a strong resemblance, even though he is older. This young man approaches us and greets us. "Hello Francoise, I am very happy to meet you. My name is Archie," and he carries on, "I have to tell you something. About three weeks ago, I woke up one morning, and I felt bizarrely, how to say it … unblocked. All the way throughout my childhood, I felt blocked; and that morning something happened. What? I don't know!"

"How old are you?" (Three weeks, the time matches exactly with the phone call with my daughter, and the evening I connected with my grandson.)

"Twenty-two years old." I tell him about my grandson. And then he opens up, he tells me all about his previous problems, bullying, shyness, etc. Listening to him, I find the same worries that my grandson has. This young Polish man continues: "That morning, when I woke up … I felt amazing so I wanted to do seminars to keep the feeling. So I went on the internet and opened the first page. There you are! Your picture. I told myself, I must meet this woman!"

So, by a coincidence that maybe is not a coincidence, I find myself face to face with Archie. I think about my grandson who is thousands of kilometres away. I won't be able to explain it. Why am I being shown this story with amazing synchronicities? Indeed, we are particles. Particles that are able to travel, so what is this energy that can link everyone?

Sometimes, I act without understanding the reasons. A source, something, comes alive within me.

Now I would like to tell you about this woman who came to one of my seminars. It sometimes happens that I spend more time with certain people. On this occasion, I start working with this woman. I start doing gestures, movement around her eyes. I tell her that on this side, the right side, she does not know where she is going. To be more precise, she does not see in which direction to go.

So with my hands, I remove 'stuff' that is bothering her. Without knowing it, I am acting on the problem she had in her eye (declared, as I find out later, inoperable by the doctors). She is at risk of losing her sight on this side. At the end of the seminar, I find myself with her again, and she is crying. She can see! The eye that was declared sick, lost … she can see again. I only told her that on that side of her life, she could not see where she was going, so obviously, she could not go on and move forward.

Since this seminar, her life has changed. She comes to my seminars on a regular basis, as an assistant, but above all, she took some serious decisions. She has now separated from her husband; following that she built up her own company. Everything seems to have lightened up in her life, well at least, the path she wishes to pursue seems now clearer.

"But how do you know? Maybe you are wrong?" Maybe ... but I 'feel'. A woman contacted me to heal her mum. "I don't believe in it at all, but I am still contacting you. Here is a photo of my mum." Upon seeing the photo of the woman, I start talking about her lungs. This is what I see. But this is not what the doctors in the hospital are saying. I am only telling you what I see. So this woman takes her mum out of the hospital and gets her into a private hospital for other tests. There, the doctor discovers that there was a misdiagnosis. She has a problem with her lungs. Her mum was then looked after. I only listen to my feelings.

A little boy has a malformation in his brain that makes him take medication every day. His mum, in a seminar with me, explains his disease, which is a real threat to his life. Not long after, she sends me a photo of her son. I don't know if there is anything I can do, but at least I can look into it. And this is what I do. I look into it.

Time passes, and then one day, she comes with her son to tell her story. Her son stopped taking medication. He is doing really well. The doctors do not understand, but he has nothing. We talk together and she asked me what I did. I see strings, poorly connected, so I reconnect them. I see things that need to be reconnected, a bit like in a computer. I take things from the space around me, I act upon things in my own way. With my hands, I make gestures. I am unable to tell you more details.

A neurologist, coming to my seminar, gave me some clues. It sometimes happens that I can see … (I am sorry, but I am missing words to be more precise) let's say … white circles, and others more like grey ones. One day, to 'reconnect' someone, I find myself blowing on the grey ones to make them go away, when I hear a voice telling me: *Cut them off. These things they grow again.*

The neurologist has other words for my vision. "The things that you are seeing correspond a priori to the thoughts sent to the brain. I believe you are influencing the thoughts, thoughts that are just crossing. So cutting them allows purification and makes more space for more thoughts that can be positive."

I take this opportunity to tell her more about the vision I have globally about the body. For this neurologist, listening to the description I give her, I perceive the nucleus of DNA. I give my explanation as best I can, specifying that I also see a little clap. There, behind this clap, she tells me, are our memories, what some of us call our ancestral memories.

For me, behind this clap, (I can only talk about myself) there is nothing. So I believe that sometimes people think they are living events, from these memories, these memories can be real or fiction. Whatever they are, most of the time, they block thoughts and retrain perspectives to move forward. These memories can be important burdens that we must learn how to get rid of.

To Connect

When I meet someone, I go inside him, or her. A yearning gets me to see further than the physical body. We are energy. More and more, I feel myself in connection, a strong connection, with space, with everything that surrounds me. This new intensity is both fascinating and scary. Fear of the unknown is present in all of us. I am now at the stage of hyper sensibility, which allows a certain communication with the universe, with everything that is alive, with everything that vibrates within that energy. If I am vigilant, if I can feel the present moment, listen, listen to myself then I can open to the unknown. Without fear!

This sensibility can be held by a whole group, because we are all connected. Each and every one of us is linked to the world, one way or another; we express it in our own way. I believe that together, we can succeed in greatness. If we learn to channel the energy in a beneficial way, then maybe the world can wake itself up.

During seminars, I often do a very simple exercise. I ask the group to feel the energy of benevolence, working in pairs. Think about things that feed this energy. After a while, the group gets together, each with the words they choose to describe that energy of benevolence.

I then ask for a volunteer to move away from the group, and I will call him/her when I see fit. While he/she is away, I work with the group, using the completely opposite technique from what we were just doing. I ask all of them to get ready for when our volunteer will come back in.

Our volunteer comes in and goes to the middle of the room. Just before, I asked for the group to send unpleasant, nasty words as soon as the volunteer came in. Not out loud, simply by thoughts in the energy. Very quickly, our poor volunteer curls up on the floor, while we are not saying anything, starts telling us to, "Stop, please stop … I am in pain." I wanted to show the resonance between thoughts and feelings, especially when we have unhealthy thoughts. The volunteer was crying. Naturally, very quickly, I was there to reassure them, and we all embrace. I was explaining while sending benevolent thoughts with the help of the group.

When we decide that a situation is serious or dramatic, we are making it more so. Thinking the opposite will not take the burden off our shoulders but it will not make it worse, it will not feed it.

Today, we can see it work very well with fear, driven and multiplied everywhere and by everyone, the radio, the television, the internet ... All the media joins together to set off continuous sirens of anguish. Fear feeds on fear. The effect of the coronavirus feeds this phenomenon. I do not deny the existence of the virus, but I am saying that it not necessary to 'fatten up' the fear around this phenomenon, fear that is nothing else than fear of dying.

On the contrary, I can choose to feed joy, I decide.

More than ever, I pick up on everything. For me today, we are starting a new chapter. The human being is about to go on a different path, to (re)connect with nature. I feel something important is about to start. I cannot say anything with more precision, but I can feel it, I perceive a movement that is starting.

My perception becomes more and more clear.

Particles

Lying down on the lawn, I become this little girl who communicates with the grass. So when Bruno tells me he is about to start cutting the grass, I reply: "Please ... just wait."

Everything is alive, I have the potential to connect myself.

Each of us has a potential. Our potentials, if they end up on the same frequency, the same vibration, will become a beautiful energy for our own good.

On the plane that is taking me east, I am contemplating the landscape by the window, the blue sky, the sea of clouds, the light, when ... all of a sudden all this beauty assails me. I feel grabbed by this performance. At this moment, as I am sitting on my seat, beauty materialises. Everything becomes particles. This big everything of beauty becomes particles. I become the landscape, the beauty of the moment. What grabs my interest is to go to unknown places, to go and meet life. I think that all my life it is what I was looking for, and continue to do so: to live the unknown. Each moment is unknown. A new discovery to explore. Each moment.

Between fear and wakening. Like a shoot of ... Not long ago, I experienced an alignment that shook me. My entourage told me that my face emanated a peaceful strength.

During a seminar, we were working on the words: tranquillity, peace and joy. There are eighty persons entering the vibration of these words. Except that, for an unknown reason, Philippe, my companion, wants to explain. And I can see that his explanation disturbs the harmonious alignment that we have established. How to describe it? I can see the strings from that privileged moment starting to bend and distend. I quickly warn Philippe, and at the same time, there is a sudden noise in the room. Boom! We keep our session going but I stay surprised by what just happened. The session is now finished, we go and have a look where the noise came from. Between two windows, the wall is cracked from ceiling to floor!

Maja reminds me that it is the second time an event like that has happened. On a more serious note, I believe that if a harmonious alignment is disturbed, unexpected events might happen.

When I feel an alignment of such power, I enter a moment of what I qualify as pure. From my face, peace emanates. I feel it. I am peaceful.

My sensibility can be developed to the point where I can enter unknown territories. During a seminar, when I go into the room, someone walks past me. Suddenly, I have the impression of having only the vision. I find myself thrown into the space that surrounds me.

I am here and I am not here. I hear everyone, all their thoughts. I am hot. People want to speak to me, but I don't understand anything. Words don't exist. I feel myself connected to everything that vibrates. I am too hot. I must go, for a moment, anchor myself to earth.

I had the feeling of being everywhere at the same time. I believe that our brain has connection that we still ignore. I believe I was completely in the moment, the present, separated from the past. In order to explain this feeling, I like to talk about our shadows. When we take a photo in sunlight, we clearly see our shadow attached to us. For me, this shadow symbolises the past, our ancient memories. And, more often than not, we tend to identify ourselves to this past that burdens us and prevents us to be in the present.

By entering this modified state of consciousness (by dissolution?), I see strings, full of colours, linking everything. I see these strings around me, some are broken, others frayed. I see. The connection with space then becomes very strong. I discover an intensity like never before.

Only the Magic of the Present

Today, when I talk about entering vibration, I first of all evoke the learning of feelings.

> Listen to yourself.
> Listen to the world.
> One does not go without the other, so much are they interlinked.
> To prevent yourself from listening can lead to catastrophe.
> To listen to yourself allow yourself to hear what vibrates inside of you.
> And to let in, in resonance, our thoughts and our being.

Silence

Know how to grant yourself these moments.

Do something that nobody in our society does anymore. Today, we are submerged by our numerous activities, and with all the tools you have to save time, we cannot stop running. We could be led to believe that the majority of our days are spent wasting time through wanting to save time. Even in our moments of pause, quick, a screen, the radio, something to keep our mind busy. We don't know how to do nothing anymore. We run, of course in a society where a god tells us money is time, and our acts of faith summarise in our consumption.

The first thing to do is to allow yourself some time and to thank yourself for taking this time, only for yourself. Do something that nobody in our society, does anymore: stop!

Know how to say stop and give yourself the right to silence. To take refuge in silence can be of great rescue.

Stop *everything* and settle down.

Close this book for two minutes in silence … you must be brave to enter the world of silence, an instant, a day, more, less … On a regular basis, to come back to the source, the silence, and draw from it. I can't promise you what you will find: pain, joy, fear, doubt, love, anger, peace? Yet, bit by bit, you will catch the essence of what animates you: joy.

This experience opens you to feel the world on a more subtle level and therefore see yourself better. Find or find it again, your own nature again. Because we are a fire, we must keep alight, this brazier lightens up our steps day after day.

Silence shelters a precious adventure deep inside our heart.

Love Yourself

The call of the soul is what urges us to look into all the beauty and the potential we have. This consciousness allows us to touch all the parts we have, in order to bring them love and compassion. In this way, we will notice a string, leading our emotions, joys and suffering, to one aim: to grow in self-love. This position is an indication of a great deliverance and an extraordinary reconciliation with our deepest darkest parts.

Feel the depth in our most difficult moments.

Love without condition. The big lesson is to learn to love yourself, without condition. The others facing me, if I don't like them, there is a reason. They are here to say something. They are mirroring a part of me that I do not like. Others are a wonderful mirror for you.

What is happening outside is, I really believe it, a reflection of what we are holding inside.

If we are waiting in our heart, a new love, we can be certain that it will come soon and we must prepare our heart for joy, to hope for this new love. A huge healing will come and leave its balm on all the wounds from the past love.

This learning process has good surprises in store for you. We must learn to welcome the hot and promising rays of this joyful sun. We must express ourselves with simplicity and joy because our inner child is ready to be loved and be surprised by life.

Life invites you to transform yourself, to change your passions into actions, to go from passive joy to active joy where the power is ... I do not believe a word exists to qualify this force. It simply is.

Thank you.

Joy is the Food of Love

When we feed our joy, we become genies. We become creative, we become 'the more' that we are, we are like superheroes! And when we are in that state, we are doing some amazing, some unbelievable things. We are evolving our conscious.

Our spirit marvels at the world's beauty. To grow, to learn and to love. Whether we are poor or rich (or in between) we are all homeless. Whoever we are and wherever we are, we are looking to go home.

Anger linked to fear can turn our spirit upside down. We must learn to recycle our anger into treasures. The fire that animates us is still there. The bird has its nest, the spider its web, the human its heart. There is always something beautiful, something good inside us. Sometimes we must dig deep to find our demons, we must fight difficult battles to recognise them and welcome them.

It is incredible what a little love can accomplish.

We have to understand that the only thing that we are keeping forever, is what we give out.

The more we give, the more we receive. We are all different and all these differences are what make our world so beautiful and rich.

Reality can be more or less than our expectancy, it is only by having the courage to make a decision, despite our doubts and fears, that we will find out. Deciding to do nothing is the proof of our lack of confidence in life's generosity, and therefore condemns us to failure.

I only speak for myself, through my own experience. I have spent years going towards myself. So much so that, like everyone else, I find myself thinking: *that's enough now* or *yes OK, that's fine, I know myself now*.

I recently recalled my stay with Thich Nhat Hanh, Vietnamese monk master, at the Village des Pruniers. Ten days of silence. Amazing. However, at the start, the third day … I scream, I yell! I cannot take it anymore, I cry. Despite everything, I still go to the meditation. And there I hear: "Bring attention to your senses, to your perceptions of the moment."

Very often, we are monopolised by a thousand things, our mind is encumbered, we are not bringing our attention to what is going on around us.

We are walking but we are somewhere else. But if we admire a lovely landscape while thinking about a VAT form we did not fill in yet, there is very little chance that happiness comes to us. I am home and busy with daily chores, and I am thinking about sorting out my photos, and also I need to fix … Stop. Stop! I know to say stop to all these thoughts coming in. And I come back to the present moment. I recentre in the present. I 'see' clearly the mind and I can control it. Now I know.

I remember the words of Thich Nhat Hanh: "Wash your dishes as if they were a baby."

How I feel in the deepest of my being, is built with the importance I grant to a total presence, a total attention to each of my actions, as simple as they can be, as though each action represents the most important thing in the world.

This attention is taking me towards the presence, and this consciousness goes far beyond; it is an attention that vibrates in all my being, engages with all my senses, my heart, my spirit, my listening. Everything.

I don't need to be a champion of wisdom to get it; simply by saying yes to the everyday life, to carry out experiences that present themselves here and now. This learning allows us to bring to the surface the positive … and joy.

The perception of our senses is like a door that has access to joy. Our bodies resonate to joy through harmony, equilibrium. When I am in tune with my heart, my spirit, when I am in that state, I relish, I amplify, from then on, I have a feeling of profound joy.

The little girl inside, my inner child, is still here, filled with wonder, such a source, and this source is permanent. I block the source every time the mind takes its place.

The question is not to know if I am happy with myself, but if I am happy with anything. I say yes, not only yes to myself, I say yes to life. Nothing is separate. If for a moment, even a short moment, the chord vibrates, I am resonating with joy. Joy of living. So, all the vibrations of eternity align themselves so that this unique moment happens.

The present is in this instant, the yes confirmed, affirmed!

Thank you. I never hesitate to say thank you to life. To kneel to the ground and thank the universe for everything it has to offer.

We Want to Change? We Have the Power Within

I believe a part of us must die, our old patterns, unload all the burdens of ancient memories. Only the present exists. When we are in full consciousness, memories do not exist anymore, and how we feel during these moments makes us vibrate. We must detach from our shadows. It is useless to throw yourself into something that does not exist yet or does not exist anymore; you are risking feeling weighed down, slowed down.

Practising 'creation' can allow us to abandon these old patterns. It is not about making a projection; this is too much linked to the restless mind. Creation can happen by feeling the good vibration. If what I feel is positive, if this feeling creates warmth inside my being, then I can feed this feeling, maintain it. I do not project, I create. And I will do with whatever is coming.

We must start by removing the thorns of the ego. Getting rid of the name and the shape, because there is nothing. See through your own understanding that everything is illusion.

Live it!

You cannot see, because your mind will not allow you. Your mind is the only obstacle that distracts you from yourself. The mind says, *yes, it is true*. Say to your mind, *no, it is not true*. Understand your mind, learn to tame it and then it will be alongside you.

When I started to teach, I made a discovery. I had an office, but I wanted something else. Then I heard: *Francoise, teach!* I had the shivers. How can I teach? What am I going to say to people? OK, stop! I imagine 'teaching' and stop all the questioning. What do I feel? I feel a warmth rising inside me, and then I feel joy. I then decide to feed this feeling, only this one. Permanently. Then I discover what happens: people are asking me to organise a seminar. But how can I? Stop. I only feed my joy and I move forward.

Especially, don't let yourself be caught by the thoughts going through you. Listen to yourself.

Know how to listen to yourself, before the mind makes words or pain. Listen. The first thing that rises from deep inside, a strong intuition, is more often than not, pushed aside. It's coming out of nowhere. We might even find it scary. The mind does not accept it. The first reaction is to run away from it.

I love my thoughts. My thoughts feed my heart. I am what I think, so I think beauty, I think joy, I think simplicity. I see and I think 'whatever I like' to bring out the best of myself. Because this, this is me!

What is my Real Need?

What do I really want? Ask yourself this simple question and assimilate it until you feel it vibrate inside. Essential and basic question: what is my real need?

Love? Wellbeing? Time? Bars of gold? Peace? Authenticity? Freedom? Now that you asked yourself the question, take the time to develop each answer. Who can bring me what I wish for?

You! And only you!

To rely on people is to give your power away. Stop relying on people in order to be saved. Only you have the power.

If I say that I can see beyond the physical body, if I can read people, the living world is like an open book, it is not a vision of the spirit. I have learnt to feel, in full consciousness and to see.

Lately, with a group, we worked on this concept through affirmation. What do I wish for myself? When the answer is: "I want to be free," I ask them to assimilate this 'I want to be free'. And depending on the persons, I see if this affirmation comes down in the body or not.

Beyond these simple words, I wish to bring you to think about this question: for you, what does it mean to be free? What stops you from being free? As the seminar progresses, I see 'cubes' coming down until they line up with the light of 'I am free'.

If you exceed your physical body, and you enter in the vibration, if you refine your senses to feel 'where you are', then you are on the right path. Listen to the words that make you vibrate, the words that makes you sparkle, the words that sizzle inside, the words that warm your soul and your body. The more you maintain them, recite them, the more you will vibrate, the more you will learn about yourself, and accordingly the more you will expand.

Listen

Listen to yourself, to your gut. I wish to listen to my feelings, I must listen: w*hat makes me vibrate?* and even if I make a mistake, I must listen to my senses. By experiencing it, I will find out if it makes me vibrate. It is a matter of learning. I developed this capacity to listen to myself. Listen to my senses. Close my eyes and listen. *What makes me cry? What bring me happiness? Listen!* And sometimes reason has no right to be present. *Listen.*

During a seminar, I can raise up the vibration by thinking. I call upon all my allies, the natural, the marvellous. I practise without asking questions. I have full trust. Sometimes I have been asked if I am not scared about maleficent energies.

If I feel unhealthy entities, I am not scared, I push them away. When I see maleficent things, I can chase them away. It happens that sometimes, with the help of some tobacco, I puff smoke to deliver someone. Under this simple puff, I have seen people tip over. I call on my allies; sometimes I feel my dad, sometimes I feel Emma. During a recent seminar, I saw four warriors for protection accompany me and the group during the entire teaching. I have no doubt.

I have no doubt, but I don't have certainty neither. I am in the moment.

I talk about vibration because I have a deep conviction anchored inside. Everything is created by sound. When you think, or have feeling, you emit a wavelength that transforms all the energy around you, and it starts vibrating at the same level. This wavelength is effectively a sound that emits beyond the human ear. Shape cannot exist without sound.

Sound is also a wonderful tool for healing.

By making our body and organs resonate to their own level of vibrations, they can heal effectively. The disease is a 'dis-ease', an imbalance of the vibrational state of the body, and because our thoughts and feelings are indeed sound wavelength, our unstable thoughts and feelings interrupt the vibrating harmony, and therefore lead to dis-ease. That is how emotional stress can lead to disease. It is oh so simple.

Knowledge goes through learning how to feel.

It is not about how to establish some big theory. But simply about being vigilant to our own emotions, to ourselves. This learning curve requires you to 'be with yourself' at all times, and at the start it is a real workout.

Listen to the things that make you vibrate. Enter into your values, your very own.

I sincerely believe that we are all vibrations, strings of all different colours.

What makes you vibrate in the universe?

Now, I know what brings me happiness. I have managed to identify those moments, it is simple for me, I feel a very specific physical sensation. I have a tingling sensation that overtakes me.

I am not a human being, I am a musical instrument and life gives me the authorisation to play her.

Words for the End and Therefore the Beginning

Silence – courage – selflove – listen – instant – vibrate. If we take in each of these words, one by one, one after the other, and we hug it close to our heart, if we choose to give our full attention to each of them, if we choose to overindulge them, like a newborn ... then, we are without a doubt entering the universe, forthwith. This magic world! We often forget about its beauty ... At every moment, we must discover.

Our being does not need to go out and meet life, we are life.

We are dazzling. Don't let yourself being entertained by all sorts of sirens, that are only here to drive you away from your true essence.

Allow yourself to believe in the magic of life. Life has a lot more resources than our simple imagination!

Silence – courage – selflove – listen – instant – vibrate. Seven methods, seven soldiers, seven wizards, seven elves... Seven words with which you can build your own prayer, your own mantra, your own chants, your own beliefs ... your own joy. *Siamecinvi! Be your own creation.*

Seven words that hold infinite treasure. I choose to discover them and cherish them, every day.

Thank you.

Postscript
When We Start To Understand Nature, Progress Is Infinite

For a few days now, I have had a feeling that something is about to happen. I don't know what. I trust in life, I observe, I listen, I ask life to put all that is fair in front of me, in the moment, for the universal cause. Woah! What I am experiencing is extraordinary. This is all my teaching, everything is possible.

I feel overwhelmed this morning. Tears of gratitude overcome me with ... I don't know. It is absolutely wonderful, it is as though life is putting all its energy, power to the thousands, to join all my wishes, for a good cause. In three days, everything is here. Boom! It is perfect, simple, easy, no shadow. Everything happens in perfection, on a platter, simply feeling the project from within, let go ...

An abundance: gifts, this energy of gratitude. My feelings are crazily precise.

That night, I wake up with a feeling of being watched, but by a benevolent watcher. And I hear: *You teach; live in the moment. Let's be creative, everything is here, everything is possible. We are sending you everything you asked for, for the good cause. Observe how you react, look at your emotions that are rising up. Even if it scares you to move towards this wonderful unknown where everything is feasible, keep on, look and transmit.*

And I fall back asleep, my thoughts go towards my projects, and I understand how my mind asks all the questions. When a noise wakes me up, I feel as if I am being watched ... I centre myself, I feel fear coming. But a fear different from the one commonly felt, a fear tainted with wonder. I feel this unknown vibration. Having a feeling of being watched, trusting, listening to all the ways that 'they' manifest themselves. *Get up and write* (it is 3am). I turn around in my bed and close my eyes. I feel a warm breath close to me: *Get up*. OK. I know that 'they' won't give up.

Integrate it all, something is about to be born, to start, you cannot prevent it from happening.

The task is big, start a project, an idea. Accept the unknown that is coming, it is now time to act, to initiate what must be. However, do not be agitated or worried.

Going to the unknown is an adventure that is happy, painful and troubling at the same time. Trust is the healing. This moment is opportune to let go of the principles that are not suited for survival.

Developing a new vision, having a new look at things. We are reaching a corner.

Crossing a river, there is no bridge! *What to do?*

Stay on the shore and wait …

Or dive in and find what you are looking for?

Yes, I know how to swim, am I scared to get into the water, to get wet?

Look for the signs. It is an invitation.

The creations are our mirror.

Appendix
Words from my Father

My father wrote me a letter before he died. I keep it like a precious gift.

"I was so proud, and I felt like a giant holding you in my arms, your eyes discovering life, the world, and I was there to show you it, to guide you, my little one.

I had so much pain to let you go, not being able to protect you. Today, I feel lost, and here you are, to show me where to go, where I know nothing.

I have so much pain leaving you today.

You did make me grow old, you made me grow.

I learnt so much from you.

I am so proud of you, stay true to yourself, live the moment and listen to your heart, we will find each other again."

My Words, My Feelings, My Vibrations

Acceptance
- Acceptance is not resignation.
- To accept also allows us to be ourselves.
- We are not here to make things perfect.
- Acceptance is unconditional.

The dance of life contributes to unity
- A perfect balance between dynamism and immobility; make your life a piece of art, of music.

Vibrate to your own wavelength
- An infinite force. Indestructible. Constant. This force has no brakes. All that resists disappears.
- From now on, I am never alone.
- I am linked to this force from within, that gives me access to the 'everything is possible' … to live this profound state can be destabilising.
- A blind truth is necessary, an absolute faith.
- The mind is like a veil hanging over the heart. And to ignore it is to ignore oneself.
- Following ancient beliefs … or welcoming everything that is given, without having any judgment. Savouring.
- Everything is OK, I am alive.
- The wavelength of the vibration is high and invites me to elevate myself towards it, at my own pace.

Other colours
- Let go of the past, step over it in order to welcome a new phase with trust.
- Continue on your path, despite the disruptions, by staying loyal and sincere to your needs … even if …
- Without regrets or resentments, to close a door forever and to open another. By expressing yourself clearly to others, the limit of the respect establishes itself naturally.

- Open yourself to love, without expectation, and without diving into the other's energy.
- Trust while keeping your power of freedom and affirmation.
- Discover other colours, other aspects of yourself, other talents that are only asking to be discovered.
- I let myself be filled with wonder like a child with a pure heart in order to find a connection with the source.
- The heart in all its purity will become the centre of the ultimate communication with my being and will allow me to touch the heart of the source.
- It is just like this, even though ...

To love life is to love oneself

My Spiritual Warrior's Prayer

- My heart is touched giving birth to a universal project, open the hearts, participate in this adventure. My heart opens up from gratitude, I am proud of what I am!
- Through faith I have in my beauty, I develop trust.
- In gentleness, I have the force.
- In silence, I walk alongside joy.
- In peace, I understand myself and I understand the world.
- In conflict, I only see one opportunity, to choose peace.
- In detachment, I am free.
- In respect of everything that is alive, I respect myself.
- In eternity, I have compassion for the nature of all things.
- In love, I accept unconditionally the evolution of others.
- In giving, I only receive.
- In freedom, I have the power.
- In my individuality, I express the divinity within.
- In helping, I give what I have become.
- I am what I am: complete, whole, infinite.
- With gratitude, overflowing from my heart from all the incredible gifts I receive, I feel and I teach my specialty: inner joy and the divine woman.

And that is so.

Milton Keynes UK
Ingram Content Group UK Ltd.
UKHW020732091123
432249UK00012B/93

9 781789 633672